CONVERTIBLE Crystal Jewelry

REVERSE IT ▪ TWIST IT ▪ WEAR IT MANY WAYS

DIANE WHITING

KB KALMBACH BOOKS

To Cliff, for your ever-present and patient support
To Susan, for your constant belief
To Dad, for your proud enthusiasm
Thank You

Kalmbach Books
21027 Crossroads Circle
Waukesha, Wisconsin 53186
www.Kalmbach.com/Books

Published in 2014
19 18 17 16 15   1 2 3 4 5

Manufactured in the United States of America

ISBN: 978-1-62700-056-7
EISBN: 978-1-62700-057-4

Editor: Erica Swanson
Book Design: Lisa Schroeder
Technical Editor: Jane Danley Cruz
Photographers: William Zuback, James Forbes

Library of Congress Control Number: 2014944777

Contents

I've always been a lover of convertible jewelry, and when Diane told me she was preparing a book on convertible jewelry, I knew it would be a must-have in any jewelry maker's library.

Just hearing the word "convertible" teases the imagination, saying "come and find the surprise." Looking through each project is as addicting as receiving a box of delicious assorted chocolates without the index: You can't stop until you've discovered what's inside every one. Each design offers one or more ingenious ways to convert its use, whether by simply attaching a beautiful pendant using a hinged bail, weaving a bracelet that reverses to a different pattern and color, or creating an extravagant crystal-and-bead long spiral strand that can be worn as a single length, doubled, turned into a lariat and embellished with detachable tassels. Diane doesn't leave out a trick.

I first met Diane in 2006 at the annual CREATE YOUR STYLE with SWAROVSKI event in Tucson in the first class I ever taught, which, as it turns out, was the first jewelry-making class Diane ever took. Diane was already a seasoned beader, and after the class we struck up a conversation and soon learned that we shared the same the same passion for convertible jewelry. It was a connection that has been a thread of our conversations ever since. Being in the same industry, our paths continued to cross, especially when we both became CREATE YOUR STYLE with SWAROVSKI ELEMENTS Ambassadors in 2009. Diane and I share many "firsts," so it is with excitement and great joy that I write this introduction to Diane's first book featuring convertible jewelry—and under the banner of Swarovski where we first met!

Whether you are an experienced jewelry artist or just getting started, this book will inspire you with beautiful projects and surprising elements that will leave you asking yourself, "why didn't I think of that?"

— Linda Hartung of Alacarte Clasps,
WireLace

Introduction

I want you to think of your jewelry the same way you think of the clothes you wear.

Look in your closet and you will probably see a couple of wardrobes consisting of individual pieces that combine in numerous ways. Whether you're dressing for work or for leisure, your wardrobe probably follows this idea: component pieces that work together. A few pairs of pants match with dozens of t-shirts, sweaters, blouses, tanks, dusters, twin sets, etc. Most of us practice the separates concept of dressing. And whether you dress for a conservative environment or a completely free artistic expression, your wardrobe will always reflect your personal style and taste because of the colors and shapes you choose.

This is also true of your jewelry!

I've been practicing this concept with my jewelry wardrobe for years, and with this book, I invite you to join me. The pieces I present here can all be worn in more than one way. Some are reversible; flip them over and you are wearing a different color version of the same design. Some can be layered; multiple strands in different colors mixed together and worn as long necklaces or doubled over or twisted into shorter versions. Some come apart and can be reassembled into two or more pieces. Some have pendants or tassels that can be attached or removed to fit your neckline or event.

All of the pieces share one common material: Swarovski Elements. My love affair with Swarovski began shortly after I learned how to make my first beaded piece (a wire-and-bead votive candle jar cover). Nothing has ever, or will ever, match their quality, consistency, and sparkle! In addition, Swarovski is constantly innovating and presenting new shapes, cuts, colors, and finishes. I never tire of designing with Swarovski Elements, and I hope that I will introduce you to some new shapes that you will also begin to love.

My designs in this book allow you to use Swarovski Elements in all your pieces. For some, you can buy one large pendant and use it with a variety of neckpieces. For example, "Tila for Two" and "Peyote Pathway" use the same crystal beads for both sides of the bracelets. The "Buttonhole Bracelet" and "Buttonhole Pendant"

allow for the filigree or button focals to be used in either a necklace or a bracelet.

This book is designed for brand-new and seasoned jewelry makers alike. Begin with the simplest and easiest projects at the front of the book, and progress to more complex pieces as you develop your skills. Most jewelry-making techniques are covered, from stringing to wirework and stitching. And you'll need just a few tools!

Create ropes and necklaces in basic colors and metals: black, gold, silver, gunmetal, rose gold, etc. Add pops of color with pendants, sliders, and tassels. Swarovski Elements pearls work in so many ways to stretch your jewelry wardrobe. Pearls are appropriate in even the most conservative environments, and crystal beads added to pearls increases the glamour! Mix, match, twist, and turn your jewelry around.

I hope you enjoy learning how to make convertible crystal jewelry. Have fun making your jewelry work as hard as you do!

Sparkles and smiles!

Before You Begin

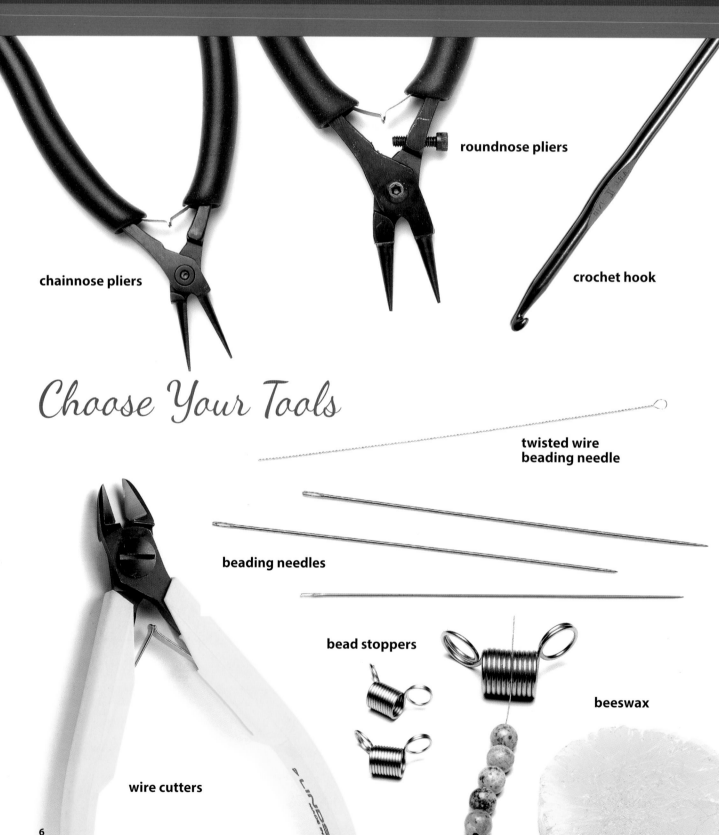

roundnose pliers

crochet hook

chainnose pliers

Choose Your Tools

twisted wire
beading needle

beading needles

bead stoppers

beeswax

wire cutters

Find the Right Materials

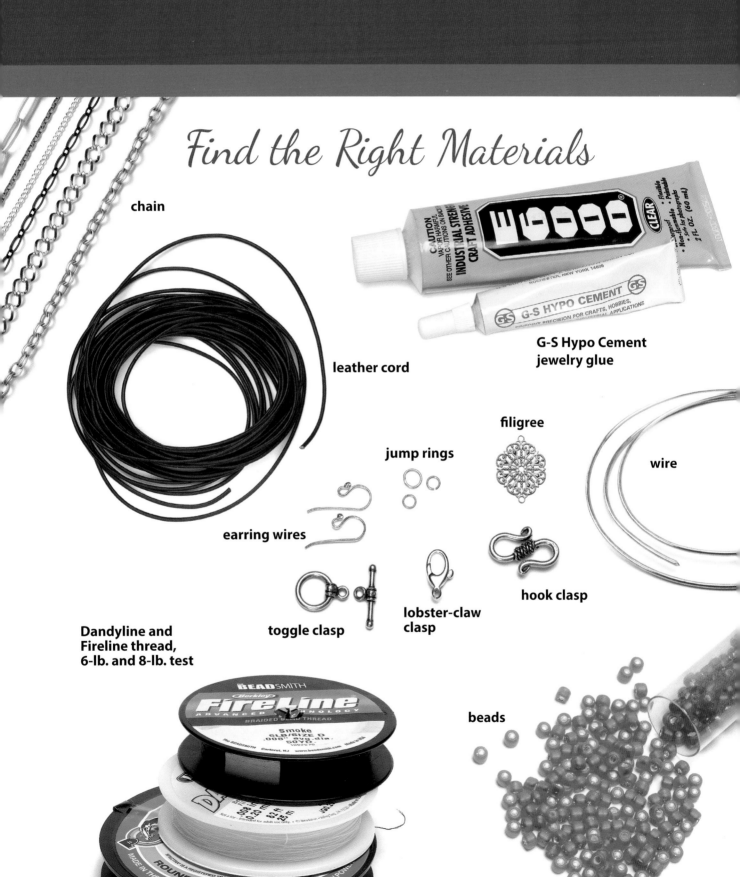

chain

leather cord

E6000 CLEAR INDUSTRIAL STRENGTH CRAFT ADHESIVE

G-S HYPO CEMENT

G-S Hypo Cement jewelry glue

filigree

jump rings

wire

earring wires

hook clasp

toggle clasp

lobster-claw clasp

Dandyline and Fireline thread, 6-lb. and 8-lb. test

beads

Crystals, Crystal Pearls, and More

ABOUT SWAROVSKI ELEMENTS

In 1895, a 33-year old Daniel Swarovski has a very big secret. So big was his secret, that he could no longer remain in his Bohemian hometown, the center of glass making and cutting for the entire European jewelry industry. It was there that Daniel had learned the art of glass cutting in his father's small company and had patented an electric cutting machine that allowed precision faceting of crystal. This was Daniel's secret. He moved his young family and his business partners to a small farming community in the Tyrolean Alps, near the city of Innsbruck. Here, he had an abundant source of water to power his electrical cutting machines, remoteness to keep his secret from competitors, and a direct rail connection to Paris, the central market for his high-quality jewelry stones.

From the beginning, innovation has been key to the Swarovski company. Twice yearly, Swarovski launches new cuts, shapes and colors to stay at the leading edge of fashion. Trend managers attend all the major runway shoes in Paris, Milan, London, and New York and work closely with fashion designers to determine upcoming trends and provide colors and cuts of stones, beads and pearls that we will all be enjoying for years to come.

Swarovski's innovation has led to a redefinition of crystal, a new DNA. Since September 2012, the entire assortment of Swarovski Elements has been switched to their new Advanced Crystal standard, an innovative lead-free crystal composition (crystal glass and all other materials containing 0.0009% lead or less,) patented in the U.S., Japan, and 16 European countries. The new formula has the same sparkle, clarity, and dependability for which Swarovski is famous.

My personal journey with Swarovski began when I was a young girl. My mother's jewelry box was a thing of wonder for me. My favorite piece was a sparkling bracelet, six rows wide of clear crystals (probably in cupchain settings.) My father brought the bracelet home from a Mediterranean cruise while in the Navy. Of course I pretended they were diamonds, and it wasn't difficult to imagine them as such—they glittered and sparkled with every turn of my wrist.

So many years later, when I first began to design purses and jewelry, I wanted to work with the best-quality materials, so there was no question that I would be using Swarovski. Whatever size, shape or color, all Swarovski Elements are precision cut and polished as to verge on perfection. I am always confident that my designs can be successfully recreated because the sizes and shapes will not vary from one element to another.

I've had so much fun experimenting with different bead shapes and playing with elements that were originally designed for another use. Here are my favorites that I've used in this book:

Flatbacks (Article series 2000)
These come in sizes as small as the head of a pin to as large as 40mm round (that's a little more than 1½ in./3.8cm). Their flat backs make them ideal for reversible pieces. While many of the styles and sizes are available with Swarovski's hot-fix adhesive, I use the ones without it.

Sew-On Stones
(Article series 3100–3700)
While these were designed for the costume and dressmaking industries, they work wonderfully in jewelry making also. Once again, the flat backs make them easy to incorporate into reversible designs.

Fancy Stones
(Article series 4100–4800)
Fancy Stones are faceted on both front and back and make excellent focal points to pendants and bracelets. Swarovski's Fancy Stones also include their Cosmic line. Squares, ovals, rounds, and rhombus shapes all have large open interiors that allow use as interchangeable pendants and components.

Beads (Article series 5000–5700)
Where would we be without the Swarovski Xilion-cut bicone or round shaped beads? The newer flat beads: rounds, ovals, mini-rounds, mini-ovals, mini-squares, mini-rectangles, pear-shaped and rhombus, all have such exciting possibilities. The Artemis beads and the new dome beads can even be used to make magnetic claps.

Pearls (Article series 5800)
Pearls go with anything—dressed up or down, they are always appropriate. These crystal pearls have a consistency of shape and size that only Swarovski can provide. And the colors…oh the colors!

Be Charmed Beads
(Article series 5900 and 80 000)
The Be-Charmed series combines large-holed metal interiors with modern faceted, pave-style or pearls. These mix and match components work great on their own to accent the slider-style pendants

Pendants (Article series 6000)
There are 78 different shapes of pendants, and too many sizes and colors to count! Most of the larger (28mm and above) have holes large enough to string leather cording or waxed thread through. I prefer using the small pendants for tassel ends. The large-holed pendants are so easily interchanged and make a dramatic statement. My three favorites are the Art-Deco inspired "Helios" pendant, the Disc Pendant, and the Olympic-inspired "Victory" pendant.

Metal Buttons and Filigree
(Article series 60 000–62 000)
These crystal encrusted metal pieces are a bit more difficult to find than most Swarovski Elements, but well worth the search. Look for them at your local bead store or at bead shows, especially the vintage vendors.

Crystal Rocks (Article series 72 000)
This strikingly modern element combines a synthetic carrier material with double pointed chatons that can be applied using hot-fix technology. They are ideal for use with textiles as well as metal components.

reverse it!

twist it!

change it up!

add a tassel!

flip it!

turn it
inside out!

Shamelessly Simple
SLIDERS

CONVERT IT!

Switch out the large focal bead for a mix-and-match look—or use a different pendant on the bottom (pull gently on the lark's head knot to open it).

a

b

c

MATERIALS
- **Swarovski Elements**

  40mm Ellipse Pendant (Article 6470) OR 30mm Cosmic Circle (Article 4139)

- 40–45mm large-hole bead

- 1 yd. (.9m) 4mm suede cord

- convertible clasp

TOOLS
- sharp scissors

- flatnose pliers

- 4–5 in. (10–13cm) 24- or 22-gauge craft wire

Slide a colorful focal bead on a leather cord for almost instant jewelry gratification!

MAKE THE SLIDER

1 Fold over one end of the suede cord 1½–2 in. (3.8–5cm). Tie an **overhand knot** (Technique Spotlight) with the folded end **(photo a)**. Use flatnose pliers, if necessary, to grip and pull the folded end through the loop. Repeat on the other end of the cord.

2 Fold the craft wire and the cord in half. Slide the wire onto the folded end of the cord.

TIP The wire helps guide your cord. You don't need it, but it's helpful when working with small holes.

3 To assemble the pendant, slide a large-hole bead over both cord ends and create a **lark's head knot** (Technique Spotlight) with the Ellipse pendant in the middle of the cord **(photos b and c)**.

4 Use a convertible clasp of your choice to join the two end loops on the cord.

TIP Try making a couple of neck cords in different lengths so the pendant fits with different outfits!

TECHNIQUE SPOTLIGHT

Making an Overhand Knot
Make a loop and pass the working end through it. Pull the ends to tighten the knot.

Making a Lark's Head Knot
String the wire through the hole in a focal, pendant, or donut to bring the folded cord through the hole. Lay the fold over the focal, and push through the center hole and down behind the bottom of the focal. Open up the fold and slide the focal back through the loop. Pull the cord ends to tighten the knot.

Sparkle
PENDANT
SLIDER

CONVERT IT!

Make dangles in different colors, or on multiple cord colors for lots of contrast. Add or remove the crystals as you like.

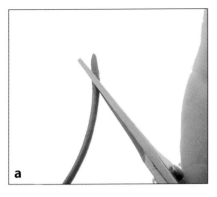
a

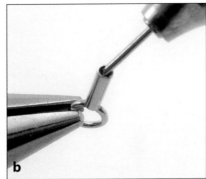
b

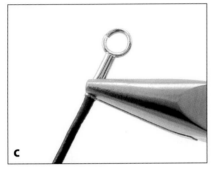
c

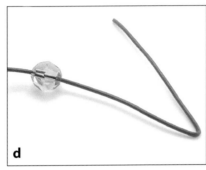
d

e

f

MATERIALS
- **Swarovski Elements**

  40mm Ellipse Pendant
  (Article 6470)

  3 8mm round crystals (Article 5000)

  3 8mm globe beads (Article 5028/4)

  9 6mm crystal briolettes
  (Article 5040)

- **2** loop crimps (Beadalon #344A-120)

- 10mm lobster-claw clasp and jump
  ring

- 2½ yd. (2.3m) 1mm leather cord

- G-S Hypo cement or jewelry glue

TOOLS
- sharp scissors

- **2** pairs of chainnose pliers

MAKE THE NECKLACE CORD

1 With sharp scissors, cut about 25 in. (64cm) of 1mm leather cord (or the desired length of your necklace minus 2 in./5cm). Re-cut both ends to a very sharp angle **(photo a)**.

2 Apply a small amount of glue to the inside of the loop crimp tube end **(photo b)**.

3 Slide one end of the cord into the tube. Using flatnose pliers, flatten the tube end to tighten it around the leather **(photo c)**. Repeat with the second loop crimp tube on the other end. Attach the lobster clasp to the crimp tube ring on one end. Set aside while the glue dries.

MAKE THE DANGLES

1 To make the first leather dangle, slide an 8mm round crystal bead on the long length of remaining cord. Fold the cord over approximately 1¾ in. (4.4cm) from the end **(photo d)**.

2 Tie an **overhand knot** (Technique Spotlight, p. 13) on the folded end. Use flatnose pliers, if necessary to grip and pull the folded end through the loop **(photo e)**. Pull the short end of the leather to tighten the knot **(photo f)**, leaving a ½-in. (1.3cm) loop, and cut the short end close to the knot. (The dangles will be approximately 1 in./2.5cm long.)

TECHNIQUE SPOTLIGHT

Opening and Closing a Jump Ring or Loop
1 Hold a loop or jump ring with two pairs of chainnose pliers.

2 To open the loop, bring the tip of one pair of pliers toward you and push the tip of the other pair away.

3 Reverse the steps to close the loop.

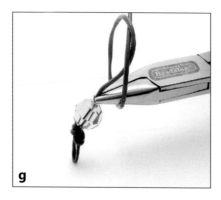

g

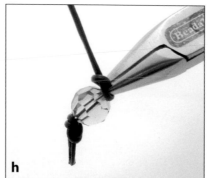
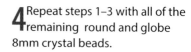

h

3 Slide the crystal bead tight against the knot, and tie an overhand knot with the long end of the cord. Using pliers or tweezers, grasp the cord close to the bead and tighten the knot. Cut the cord close to the knot **(photos g–i)**.

i

j

4 Repeat steps 1–3 with all of the remaining round and globe 8mm crystal beads.

5 Repeat steps 1–3 with the 6mm briolettes, except make one grouping of three briolettes and three groupings of two briolettes **(photo j)**.

ASSEMBLY

1 Attach the crystal pendant to the center of the necklace cord with a **lark's head knot** (Technique Spotlight, p. 13) **(photos k–m)**.

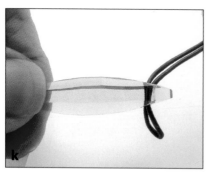

k

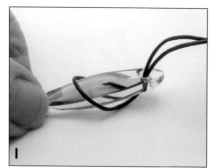

l

2 Slide a three-bead and a two-bead dangle down to the pendant on each side of the neck cord. Bring both sides of the neck cord together and slide the remaining dangles (as few or as many as you like) over both cords and down to the pendant **(photos n, o)**.

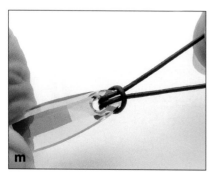

m

n

o

Simply Strung
NECKLACE

CONVERT IT!

Wear the strands long, or make a knot in front. For a short, twisted necklace: Group five or six strands, slip a twister clasp on one end, twist, and connect the other end with the clasp. You can also wrap a few strands around your wrist for an easy bracelet.

About Twister Clasps
A twister clasp is perfect for connecting—and re-connecting—lots of strands together in creative ways. You'll find these versatile clasps at your favorite bead store or online in many finishes and sizes.

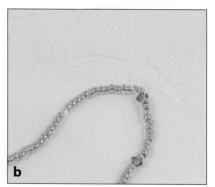

Seed beads and crystals strung on continuous strands are super-easy and totally versatile. Use any small accent beads you like, including pearls, crystals, and gemstones, to make tons of different strands.

DETERMINE YOUR LENGTH
Use a tape measure to measure around your wrist comfortably (not tight). Multiply your wrist measurement by six. This measurement will be the finished length of your long necklace. The total length is between 42–52 in. (1.07–1.32m).

STRING THE NECKLACE
1 Cut 2 yd. (1.8m) of thread, and thread the needle (pull only about 2–3 in./5–7.6cm of thread past the eye). Measure approximately 2–3 in. from the needle, and mark with a colored marker or pen. From that point, measure your personal length and mark the other thread end **(photo a)**.

2 Attach a **bead stopper** to the end mark on the thread (Technique Spotlight), and string an alternating pattern of 15 11º seed beads and a 3mm crystal until the area between the two marks is filled with beads.

TIP Cull your 11ºs for a smooth and uniform look: Pick through the beads and discard any that are broken, misshapen, or oddly colored. Plan on using at least 25 percent more beads when you cull.

3 Bring the two marks together, remove the bead stopper, and tie the ends together with a **surgeon's knot** (Technique Spotlight) **(photo b)**. Make sure there are no gaps between the beads.

4 Apply a drop of glue to the knot and to about ¼ in. (6mm) of the working thread, and then sew through the first two or three beads again to hide the knot. Remove the needle from that end.

5 Attach the needle to the tail, and add a drop of glue onto the thread close to the knot. Sew through the last two or three beads.

6 Let the glue dry, and then trim the thread ends close to the 11ºs.

7 Repeat as steps 1–6 many times as desired for a multistrand piece.

Change It Up!

There are so many variations of crystal beads and seed beads you can try, and the more you make, the more options you have for wearing. Here are just a few:

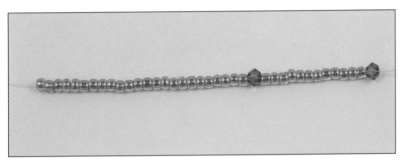

• String 24 11ºs, a 3mm bicone crystal, 12 11ºs, and a 3mm bicone. Repeat as desired.

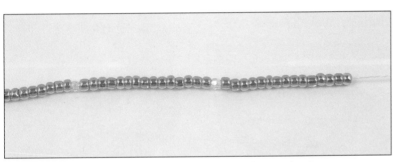

• Alternate stringing 12–18 11ºs and a 2mm round crystal. 11ºs are approximately 2mm, so a 2mm crystal will take up the same amount of space as an 11º.

• Alternate stringing 15 11ºs and a cluster (a 3mm bicone, an 11º, a 3mm round, an 11º, and a 3mm bicone).

• String an all-11º strand in one or multiple colors. This is a great way to use up your "bead soup" beads.

• Play with color and/or crystal combinations. The more you make, the more you will want to make!

MATERIALS (PER STRAND)
- **Swarovski Elements**

    60 2mm crystal rounds (Article 5000)

    OR **48–50** 3mm crystal rounds (Article 5000)

    OR **48–50** 3mm crystal bicones (Article 5328)

- 5–6 grams 11º seed beads in various colors

- beading thread, .011 in. (Dandyline)

- 20mm twister clasp

- GS Hypo-Cement or jewelry glue

TOOLS
- size 12 beading needle

- tape measure

- bead stopper

- sharp scissors or cutters

- colored marker or pen

TECHNIQUE SPOTLIGHT

Making a Surgeon's Knot
Use this knot to tie two cord ends together. Cross the right end over the left end, and go through the loop. Go through again. Pull the ends to tighten. Cross the left end over the right end and go through once. Pull the ends to tighten.

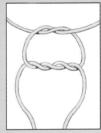

Attaching a Bead Stopper
Bead stoppers hold a long strand in place. String a beading wire through the coils on the bead stopper, and your necklace or bracelet won't go anywhere.

Ribbons and Sparkles
NECKLACE

CONVERT IT!

Add or subtract as many ribbon strands as you like when you use a multi-clasp.

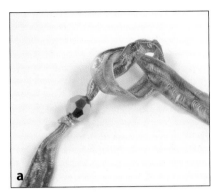

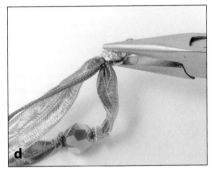

MATERIALS (5 STRANDS)
- **Swarovski Elements**

    5–14 8mm crystal round beads, 5 or 7 per strand (Article 5000)

    5–14 8mm crystal mini round beads, 5 or 7 per strand (Article 5052)

    5–14 10x8mm crystal mini oval beads, 5 or 7 per strand (Article 5051)

- 12–15 yd. (11–13.7m) ⁵⁄₁₆-in. Kujaku, Isuki, or other ribbon

- **8–10** 7mm clamshell end caps with split rings, **2** per strand

- pair of multistrand connectors with jump rings (mcleesjewelry design.com)

- lobster claw clasp

- **2** 4mm jump rings

- G-S Hypo Cement or jewelry glue

TOOLS
- twisted wire beading needle

- sharp scissors or cutters

- flatnose pliers

MAKE A THREE-RIBBON STRAND

1 Cut a 1-yd. (.9m) length of ribbon, and thread a twisted wire needle on one end.

2 String 5 or 7 crystals (rounds, mini rounds, or mini oval beads), and center them on the ribbon. Remove the needle.

3 Leave the middle crystal in the center, and slide the other crystals to the right and left of it by 3–4 in. (7.6–10cm). Tie an **overhand knot** (Technique Spotlight, p. 13) on the left side of the center crystal, and use your fingers to snug it close to the crystal. Repeat on the right side of the center crystal, making sure to move the knot close to the bead before tightening **(photos a and b)**.

4 Measure about 2½ (6.4cm) to the right of the center crystal, and tie an overhand knot. Slide the closest crystal next to the knot, and tie an overhand knot on the other side. Repeat with all of the crystals to the right of the center crystal.

5 Repeat step 4 with all of the crystals to the left of the center crystal.

6 Cut two pieces of ribbon the same length as the finished beaded strand. Group all three ribbons together, and tie an overhand knot at the very end of the strands. Cut the ends right against the knot **(photo c)**.

7 Apply glue to the inside of the clamshell end cap, and position it over the knot. Squeeze the clamshell closed with flatnose pliers **(photo d)**. Let the glue dry.

8 Smooth the ribbons so they are all the same length. Repeat steps 6 and 7 for the available ends of the ribbon. **Attach a jump ring** (Technique Spotlight, p. 15) to each clamshell ring.

9 Repeat steps 1–8 as many times as desired (I made a total of five three-ribbon strands).

ASSEMBLY

Attach a lobster claw clasp to one multistrand connector using a 4mm jump ring. Attach a 4mm jump ring to the other connector. String the desired number of three-ribbon strands on the multistrand connectors.

TIP Make a couple of ribbon-only strands to mix with the crystal strands for a more casual look—or add more crystals for even more sparkle!

Not-So-Naughty Knots
NECKLACE

CONVERT IT!

Loop a few long strands over your neck, or twist the strands together and clasp.

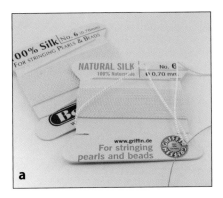

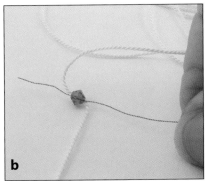

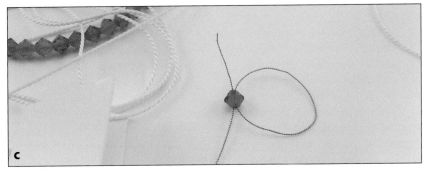

MATERIALS (5 STRANDS)

- **Swarovski Elements**

  50 4mm crystal bicone beads in each of **5** colors (Article 5328)

- **5** cards of silk thread with attached needle

- G-S Hypo Cement or jewelry glue

- twister clasp

TOOLS

- sharp scissors or cutters

- awl, tweezers, or bead knotting tool

TECHNIQUE SPOTLIGHT

Using a Stop Bead

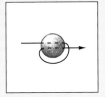

Use a stop bead to secure beads temporarily when you begin stitching. (You may want to choose a bead that is distinctly different from the beads in your project.) String the stop bead about 6 in. (15cm) from the end of your thread, and go back through it in the same direction. If desired, go through it one more time for added security.

Knotting can be easy and fun, once you find the most comfortable tool and technique. There are multiple ways to tie knots: You can use tweezers, an awl, or a bead knotting tool.

CONDITION THE SILK CORD

The silk cord will come off the card with creases, so it needs to be conditioned so it lies smooth and straight **(photo a)**. First, remove the silk cord from card (leave the needle on the cord). Wet your fingers with water. Starting near the fixed needle, pull the cord through your fingers to wet and stretch the entire strand. As you are stretching, untwist the cord just a bit; this relaxes the cord and prevents further stretching once the necklace is complete. You can also wet the cord under running water. The silk will dry very quickly.

STRING AND KNOT THE BEADS

1 Use the twisted wire needle that comes with the silk cord (or thread a new needle, if necessary). Pick up a 4mm crystal, and slide it down to within 3 in. (7.6cm) of the silk cord end. Sew through the first crystal again in the same direction **(photo b)**. The cord will loop around the crystal and create a stop bead. Pull the cord snug.

2 Tie an **overhand knot** on the cord (Technique Spotlight, p. 13) within 1 in. (2.5cm) of the first crystal. String 50 crystals on the cord as desired. I used a single color for each strand.

3 Secure all of the crystals on the cord by sliding the last crystal up to the twisted wire needle. Bend the needle to loop around the crystal, and thread through the crystal again, as you did with the first crystal **(photo c)**. Pull the twisted wire needle loop snug around the crystal.

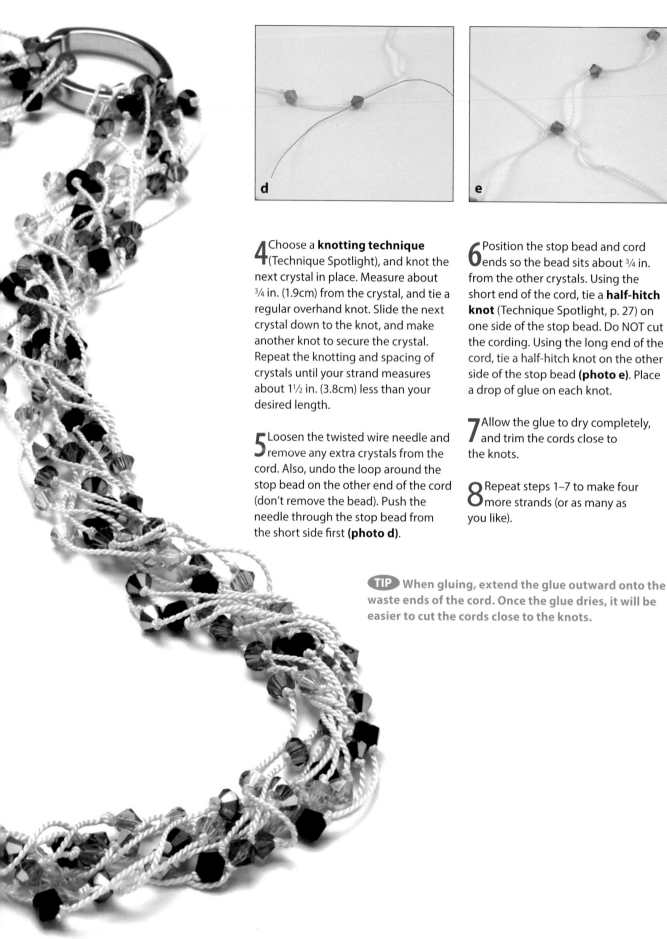

d

e

4 Choose a **knotting technique** (Technique Spotlight), and knot the next crystal in place. Measure about ¾ in. (1.9cm) from the crystal, and tie a regular overhand knot. Slide the next crystal down to the knot, and make another knot to secure the crystal. Repeat the knotting and spacing of crystals until your strand measures about 1½ in. (3.8cm) less than your desired length.

5 Loosen the twisted wire needle and remove any extra crystals from the cord. Also, undo the loop around the stop bead on the other end of the cord (don't remove the bead). Push the needle through the stop bead from the short side first **(photo d)**.

6 Position the stop bead and cord ends so the bead sits about ¾ in. from the other crystals. Using the short end of the cord, tie a **half-hitch knot** (Technique Spotlight, p. 27) on one side of the stop bead. Do NOT cut the cording. Using the long end of the cord, tie a half-hitch knot on the other side of the stop bead **(photo e)**. Place a drop of glue on each knot.

7 Allow the glue to dry completely, and trim the cords close to the knots.

8 Repeat steps 1–7 to make four more strands (or as many as you like).

TIP When gluing, extend the glue outward onto the waste ends of the cord. Once the glue dries, it will be easier to cut the cords close to the knots.

Knotting with an Awl

1 Slide a crystal close to the first knot in the work. Make a new loose overhand knot on the other side of this crystal, and pull it close to the new crystal, keeping the loop loose.

2 Place the awl point inside the loop and right next to the crystal **(photo a)**. Pull on the working end of the silk cord until the knot and the crystal are tight against the awl. Pinch the cord tightly on the side of the knot that's not against the crystal, and push the knot toward the crystal as you remove the awl.

Knotting with Tweezers

1 Slide a crystal close to the first knot in the work. Make a new loose overhand knot on the other side of this crystal, and pull it close to the new crystal, keeping the loop loose.

2 Place the tweezers inside the loop, and grab the cord where it exits the crystal **(photo b)**. Pull on the long end of the silk cord until the knot is tight up against the crystal. Pinch the cord tightly on the side of the knot that's not against the crystal, and push the knot toward the crystal as you remove the tweezers.

Knotting with a Bead Knotting Tool

1 Slide a bead close to the first knot in the work. Make a new loose overhand knot on the other side of this bead, and pull it close to the new crystal, keeping the loop loose.

2 Grasp the knotting tool with your thumb resting against the top lever. Slide the pointed section of the tool inside the loop **(photo c)**. Pull the long end of the cord with your other hand, and place it into the V-shaped section of the tool.

3 Pull the knot tight, and then push the lever up to tighten the knot against the bead and release the tool.

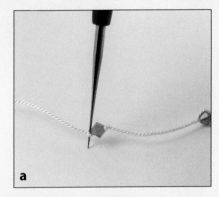

a

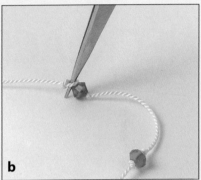

b

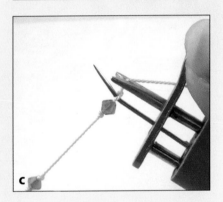

c

TIP If you want the spaces between beads to be the exact same distance, make a measuring card by cutting the silk cord card into a ¾x1-in. (1.9x2.5cm) square and folding it in half. Position this card on the cord after tightening a knot next to a bead. Make the new knot snug up against the card.

Multi-Pearls NECKLACE

CONVERT IT!

Wear any of the graduated strands individually or together. Try making another center strand in a different color for real mix-and-match possibilities.

a

b

c

MATERIALS (PENDANT)
- **Swarovksi Elements**

  27mm crystal fancy stone (Article 1201)

  121 3mm crystal pearls (Article 5810)

- 1.5 grams 11º seed beads

- 1 gram 15º seed beads

- **2** 45mm metal filigree rings (dianewhitingdesigns.com)

- 35mm metal filigree disk (dianewhitingdesigns.com)

- 20mm metal filigree oval

- beading thread, 6 lb. test (Fireline)

- wax or conditioner

TOOLS
- beading needle, size 11 or 12

- flatnose pliers

- roundnose pliers

- beading mat

- awl (optionla)

BEZEL THE FANCY STONE

1 Thread a needle on a comfortable length of beading thread (about 1 yd./.9m), and pick up a 3mm pearl and six 11º seed beads. Sew through all of the beads to make a circle, and tie two **overhand knots** (Technique Spotlight, p. 13), leaving a 6-in. (15cm) tail. Sew through the pearl and the first two 11ºs. You have made the first **right-angle weave** unit (Technique Spotlight, p. 49).

2 Pick up four 11ºs and a pearl, and sew down through the first two 11ºs in the previous right-angle weave unit and the four new 11ºs added in this step. You have completed the second (counter-clockwise) right-angle weave unit.

3 Pick up a pearl and four 11ºs, and sew up through the last two 11ºs in the previous right-angle weave unit. Sew through the new pearl and the first two 11ºs added in this step. You have made the third (clockwise) right-angle weave unit.

4 Repeat steps 2 and 3, alternating between counter-clockwise and clockwise right-angle weave units, to make a row with 18 pearls across the top, ending with a counter-clockwise right-angle weave unit **(photo a)**. Then sew (from right to left) through the top pearl.

5 Pick up three pearls, and sew through the pearl in the first row (from left to right) and then up through the first new pearl added in this step (clockwise unit).

6 Pick up two pearls, and sew from left to right through the next pearl in the first row and then up through the side pearl in the previous right-angle weave unit on this row. Continue in the same direction through the next two pearls added in this step, and the following pearl in the next right-angle weave unit in the previous row (counter-clockwise unit).

7 Continue alternating between clockwise and counter-clockwise right-angle weave units across the row, **ending** and **adding thread** as needed (Technique Spotlight, p. 37). Finish with a counter-clockwise unit with thread exiting the final pearl between the two rows **(photo b)**.

8 Join the ends of the strip to form a ring: Pick up a pearl and sew through the side pearl in the first right-angle weave unit on the other end. Pick up a pearl, and sew through the pearl your thread exited at the start of this step. Pull tight. Sew through the first pearl added in this step and the adjacent two 11ºs in the first row. Pick up two 11ºs, and sew through the corresponding two 11ºs on the other end of the first row **(photo c)**. Sew back through the first pearl added in this step.

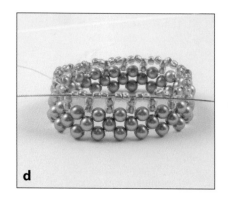

d

e

f

g

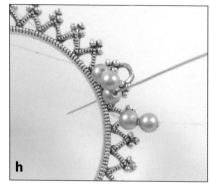

h

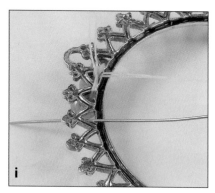

i

9 Continue through the next four 11ºs to be in position for the next step. Your thread will be exiting an 11º along the edge of the ring.

10 Sew through all the 11ºs along the edge of the ring, and pull snug so the 11ºs lie close to each other **(photo d)**. Retrace the thread path again, and continue through two 11ºs to tighten the circle and form a cup. Sew through the beadwork to exit a pearl along the opposite edge of the ring.

11 Place the fancy stone into the cup, with the back of the stone against the 11ºs **(photo e)** and the pearls along the front of the stone. Pick up a 15º seed bead, and sew through the next pearl along the top edge. Repeat, adding 15ºs between each pearl along the top edge, pulling tight to secure the stone. Retrace the thread path through all the 15ºs and the pearls again, pulling tight. Sew down through an adjacent pearl, then across through a pearl on the bottom and two adjacent 11ºs. Tie

two half-hitch knots, and sew through five or six 11ºs in the bottom ring. End the thread and set the bezelled stone aside **(photo f)**.

MAKE THE FILIGREE FRAME

1 Thread a needle on a new length of doubled and **waxed thread** (about 1 yd.) (Technique Spotlight, p. 62), and sew (from back to front) through a triangle space in the filigree frame ring, leaving about a 3-in. (7.6cm) tail. Pick up three pearls, and sew from front to back through the next triangle space to the right to make a picot shape (make sure to hold onto the tail thread). Using the tail and working ends of the thread, tie a **square knot** (Technique Spotlight, p. 27) **(photo g)**. Sew from back to front through the next empty triangle space to the right.

2 Pick up two pearls, and sew from front to back through the third pearl added in step 1 and the triangle space **(photo h)**. Pull tight to the back. Sew from back to front through the next empty triangle space.

3 Repeat step 2 around the filigree. After the last triangle space has been filled, sew up through the first triangle space and the first pearl added. Pick up a pearl, and sew down through the previous pearl and the triangle space **(photo i)**. Slip your needle under a thread, and tie a half-hitch knot. Trim one of the threads close to the filigree, and complete the remaining steps with a single thread. Sew back up through the first triangle space and pearl.

COMBINE THE PIECES

1 Lay the filigree disk right-side up on the back side of the filigree ring you just embellished. Cover the disk with the other filigree ring, making sure both pendant loops are aligned. Hold all the pieces together in your non-dominant hand.

2 Pick up a 15º, and sew back down through the same pearl and triangle space your thread exited in step 3 of "Make the Filigree Frame." You will stitch through the triangle-shaped spaces on the two frames, and capture the disk filigree between

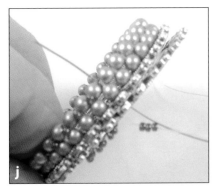

them. Pick up three 15⁰s, and sew up through the next triangle space and pearl.

3 Repeat step 2 around the entire ring, adding one 15⁰ on the front and three 15⁰s on the back (**photo j**). Finish by sewing through the first 15⁰ added in step 16 and through the pearl and filigree rings to bring the thread to the back.

4 Sew through the 15⁰s on the back of the ring (**photo k**). If needed, lift the beads into place with a needle or an awl. Continue through the first three 15⁰s, and pull the thread to make a smooth ring of seed beads. Sew back through the triangle spaces of both filigree rings, the pearl, and then sew (from left to right) through a pearl on the top round.

5 Working clockwise, sew through all the pearls on the top round. Keep the thread tension loose for now.

6 Position the bezelled fancy stone in the center of the pearl ring. Pull the thread to tighten the pearls down around the inner ring of pearls on the fancy stone. Sew through all of the pearls in the ring again, pulling tight each time, to secure. Sew down through a pearl and the filigree rings, and tie a half-hitch knot. Sew through several beads on the back side, and tie another half-hitch knot. Sew through a few more beads, and end the threads.

MAKE AND ATTACH THE BAIL

1 Grasp the filigree oval in the center using roundnose pliers. Using flat-nose pliers, gently form the oval into a curved bail shape, keeping the two narrow ends slightly separated.

2 Thread a needle on a new short length of thread (about 12 in./30cm), pick up 10 15⁰s, and then sew through the space at one end of the oval filigree piece. Sew back through the 15⁰s, and sew through both pendant filigree loops and the other end of the oval filigree. Sew back through six 15⁰s.

3 Pick up four 15⁰s, and sew through the first end of the oval filigree. Sew through two middle 15⁰s of the first 10–15⁰ group. Pick up four 15⁰s, and sew through the other end of the oval filigree. Tie a half-hitch knot, and sew through three or four 15⁰s. End the thread.

Combine It!

Follow the instructions for the "Simply Strung Necklace" to create pearl-and-crystal strands to complement your pendant. Close with a convertible clasp.

Sparkle Slip-On EMBELLISHMENT

CONVERT IT! Slide the pendant on the rope to wear it single, or fold the rope in half, attach a crystal donut with **a lark's head knot** (Technique Spotlight, p. 13), and slide the embellishment over both ends of the rope. The pendant will fit over a doubled length of rope, so be creative!

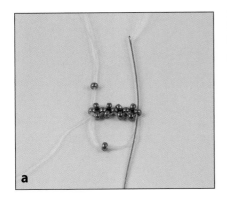

MATERIALS

- **Swarovski Elements**

    40mm Helios pendant (Article 6040)

    3mm Xilion bicone crystals
    (Article 5328)

    144 color A

    48 color B

- 30 grams 11º seed beads (1–1½ tubes)

- beading thread, 6 lb. test (Fireline)

- pearl shortener clasp

TOOLS

- size 12 beading needle

- size 10, big-eye, or twisted wire
  beading needle

- sharp scissors or cutters

- permanent marker

- toothpick or coffee straw (optional)

- beading mat

A right-angle weave tube is the perfect backdrop for slip-on pendants. You can even use this versatile embellishment with some of the other projects in this book!

MAKE THE ROPE

1 Thread a needle on a comfortable length of doubled thread (about 1 yd./.9m), and stitch a **right-angle weave** row four units long with 11º seed beads (Technique Spotlight, p. 49), leaving a 6-in. (15cm) tail.

2 To join: Pick up an 11º, and sew up through the vertical 11º at the starting end. Pick up an 11º, and sew down through the 11º your thread exited at the start of this step **(photo a)**. Continue through the first 11º added and the vertical 11º to make a tube.

TIP Starting the tube with doubled thread helps the 11ºs "stand up" in their proper positions. If you prefer to work with a single thread, you can cut one of the threads after starting the second round of right-angle weave in step 5.

3 To make the end loop, sew from left to right through the top right 11º. Pick up nine 11ºs, and sew from left to right through the third horizontal 11º (counting either left or right). Sew back though all nine new 11ºs, and then sew from left to right through the original horizontal 11º **(photo b)**.

TIP Insert a toothpick or small coffee straw into the center of the tube to support and make it easier to see the beads and stitches.

4 Sew through all five of the horizontal 11ºs twice to tighten the end just enough to fit the support. To position your thread for a new round: Sew through the closest vertical 11º and an adjacent horizontal 11º. Turn the work over so the loop is on the bottom. New rounds will be added to the open end.

c

d

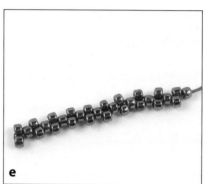

e

f

Waxing or Conditioning Thread

Use either beeswax or micro-crystalline (not candle wax or paraffin) to condition nylon thread. Beeswax smooths the nylon fibers and adds tackiness that will stiffen your beadwork slightly. Stretch the thread, then pull it through the conditioner, starting with the end that comes off the spool first.

Working Even-Count Peyote Stitch

Pick up an even number of beads (a–b). These beads will shift to form the first two rows. To begin row 3, pick up a bead, skip the last bead strung in the previous step, and sew through the next bead in the opposite direction (b–c). For each stitch, pick up a bead, skip a bead in the previous row, and sew through the next bead, exiting the first bead strung (c–d). The beads added in this row are higher than the previous rows and are referred to as "up-beads."

For each stitch in subsequent rows, pick up a bead, and sew through the next up-bead in the previous row. To count peyote stitch rows, count the total number of beads along both straight edges.

5 Pick up three 11ºs, and make a right-angle weave unit off of the previous round to start a new round. Add three more right-angle weave units, then join by picking up an 11º, sewing down through the first vertical 11º in the round, sewing from left to right though the horizontal 11º in the previous round, and then sewing up through the final vertical 11º in this round. Sew from left to right through the first horizontal 11º on the top of this new round (**photo c**).

6 Continue adding rounds of right-angle weave until you reach the desired length (44–45 in./1.1–1.2m for a long, doubled rope and 22–24 in./56–61cm for a short, single rope), **ending and adding thread** as needed (Technique Spotlight, p. 37). Finish with thread exiting a vertical 11º.

7 Repeat step 2 to make an end loop. Sew through three or four right-angle weave units, and tie a half-hitch knot. Sew through a few more right-angle weave units, tie another knot, and sew through one more 11º. End the threads.

MAKE THE EMBELLISHMENT

1 For a bead tube, I like to start with a two-needle technique: Thread a needle with 2–3 yd. (1.8–2.7m) of thread. Double the thread, and **wax** (Technique Spotlight). Thread both tail ends through another needle, leaving a very short tail (about 1½ in./3.8cm) on this end.

TIP Use a size 10, a big-eye, or a twisted wire needle to make threading the double ends easier.

2 With the first needle, pick up two 11ºs on the long end and move to within 3–4 in. (7.6–10cm) of the second needle. Pick up an 11º with the second needle, and pass it through the second 11º on the long end. Pull both threads tight (**photo d**), which will align the 11ºs to make a row of two side-by side on the bottom and one positioned between the two on the top (you now have two rows started).

3 Pick up two 11ºs on the first needle, and one 11º on the second needle. Pull all the 11ºs down to nest next

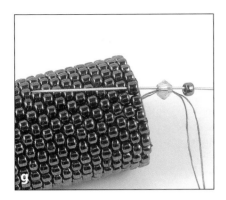

to the other 11ºs. With the second needle, sew through the second 11º on the first thread.

4 Repeat step 2 for a total of 20 rows, counting the "up" and "down" beads across to determine length **(photo e)**. Remove the needle from the short end and turn the work so the tail and working ends of the thread are on the bottom. Work in **even-count peyote** stitch (Technique Spotlight) until the work measures 24 rows.

TIP Slide the work over a bead tube while connecting the edges and adding the crystals.

5 **Zip up** the edges of the tube (Technique Spotlight, p. 55) **(photo f)**.

6 To embellish the edge, notice where the thread is exiting a bead on one end of the tube, and pick up a color A 3mm bicone crystal and an 11º. Skip the 11º, and sew back though the A and the next end 11º immediately to the right **(photo g)**.

TIP To ensure that you begin the embellishment row in the correct position on the opposite side, mark the spacing now to correspond with the first A added in step 6. Use a pen or permanent marker on the threads between the appropriate 11ºs.

7 Sew up through the next end 11º. Pick up an A and an 11º, skip the 11º, and sew back though the A and the next end 11º.

8 Repeat step 7 all the way around the tube, adding a total of 12 As. Step down for the next round by sewing downward through the bead to the immediate left on the row below the row you just finished. Then sew up through the right-side 11º on the new row **(photo h)**.

9 Pick up an A and an 11º, skip the 11º, and sew back through the A and the next end 11º on the second row. The new A will sit in between two As on the top row. Repeat this step to complete the round (12 crystals added), and step down as you did in step 8.

10 For the third round, pick up a color B 3mm bicone crystal and an 11º. Work as in step 9, adding 12 Bs. Finish by stepping down to the fourth row as before.

11 For the fourth round, pick up an A and an 11º. Work as in step 9 to add 12 As to this round. Sew through a few beads, and end the threads.

12 On the other end of the tube, attach a new 1-yd. length of doubled thread by weaving through a few end 11ºs, exiting the 11º marked after step 6. Repeat steps 6–11 to embellish this end.

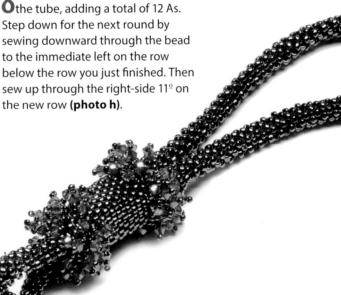

Combine It!

Change out the simple crystal pendant for a "Reversible Circle Pendant," p. 53. There are so many ways to mix and match pieces—you'll be surprised at the number of new looks you can create!

Pearl Slip-On PENDANT

CONVERT IT!

Slide this pendant onto three "Simply Strung Necklace" strands, p. 17, and use a twister or pearl shortener clasp to wear as a focal bead. Clip a tassel to the end for even more variety.

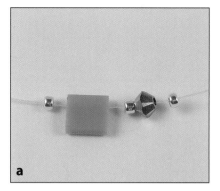

a

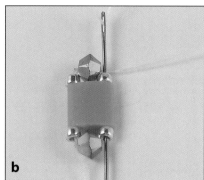

b

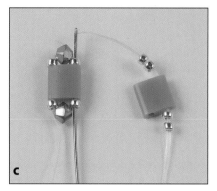

c

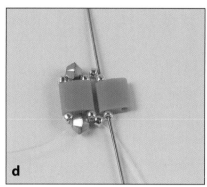

d

MATERIALS

BRACELET
- **Swarovski Elements**

    64 3mm Xilion bicone crystals (Article 5328)

    Or **64** 3mm round crystals (Article 5000)

- **32** Tila beads in each of **2** colors: A, B

- 3 grams 15º seed beads

NECKLACE
- **Swarovski Elements**

    62–70 3mm Xilion bicone crystals (Article 5328) OR 3mm round crystals (Article 5000)

    62–70 4mm Xilion bicone crystals (Article 5328) OR 4mm round crystals (Article 5000)

- **62–70** Tila beads in each of **2** colors: A, B

- 6 grams 15º seed beads

BOTH PROJECTS
- pearl enhancer clasp

- beading thead, 6 lb. test (Fireline)

TOOLS
- size 11 or 12 beading needle

- sharp scissors

- beading mat

No hint of the second side shows when you wear this elegant and feminine bracelet and necklace. The flat Tila beads are comfortable, and just a few crystal accents make this piece very affordable.

MAKE THE BRACELET

1 Thread a needle on a comfortable length of beading thread (about 1 yd./.9m), and pick up a 15º seed bead, a color A Tila bead, a 15º, a 3mm bicone crystal, and a 15º **(photo a)**, leaving a 6-in. (15cm) tail.

2 Sew through the second hole of the A, and then pick up a 15º and a crystal. Tie a **square knot** (Technique Spotlight, p. 27) with the working thread and tail, and sew in a clockwise direction through all the beads except the last crystal added. Pull the thread tight, and adjust the beads if needed **(photo b)**.

3 Pick up two 15ºs, an A, and two 15ºs, and sew down through the 15º at the top of the previous A, the A, and the 15º at the base **(photo c)**. Sew up through the two new 15ºs, an A, and a 15º (on the top of the second A). Pull the thread tight, adjusting the 15ºs so they sit at right angles to each other **(photo d)**.

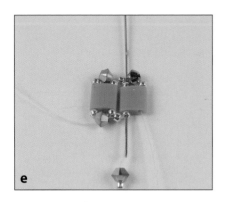

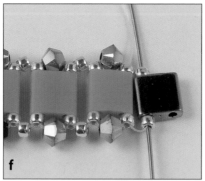

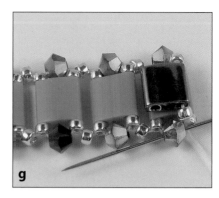

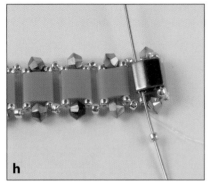

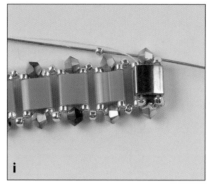

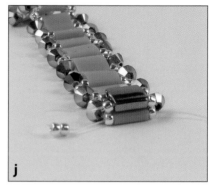

4 Pick up a crystal and a 15º, and sew down through the second hole of the A. Pick up a 15º and a crystal, and sew up through the previous 15º-A-15º **(photo e)**. Continue through the first crystal and the 15º-A-15º. Pull the thread tight, and adjust the crystals and 15ºs to lie perpendicular to each other.

5 Work as in steps 3 and 4 until the bracelet is approximately 30 As long, **ending** and **adding thread** as needed (Technique Spotlight, p. 37). Check the length for fit, and add more beads by repeating the step 2 and 3 pattern until you reach the desired length (31–35 Tilas).

6 Pick up a 15º, a color B Tila, and a 15º. Sew down through the previous 15º-A-15º, and retrace the threadpath through all the new beads. The thread will exit the last 15º added in this step **(photo f)**. Note that this is where the bracelet turns to work on the double side, so there is no third 15º in this step.

7 Flip your work and hold it in your non-dominant hand, with the thread exiting the 15º on the bottom. From right to left, sew through the crystal **(photo g)**. Pick up a 15º, and sew up through the B **(photo h)**.

8 Pick up a 15º, and sew from left to right through the crystal on the top of the two Tilas **(photo i)**. Sew through the 15º, B, and 15º on the right side again.

9 Pick up two 15ºs, and sew up through the 15º, A, and 15º behind the new B. These two new 15ºs will be positioned side by side under the 15ºs at the base of each Tila, and your thread will exit the 15º at the top of the A **(photo j)**. Pick up two 15ºs, and sew down through the 15º, B, and two 15ºs at the bottom. Flip the work so the thread is exiting a 15º at the top and to the right.

10 Pick up two 15ºs, sew down through a 15º on the left, sew back up through the 15º on the right, and continue through the first new 15º. You have now completed a **ladder stitch** (Technique Spotlight, p. 47). Repeat this step eight more times; the ladder will be a total of 11 15ºs long, and your thread will be exiting on the right-side bead **(photo k)**.

11 To join: Sew down through the 15º on the bottom right side, and then sew up through the 15º on the left side, through the ladder stitch 15º on the left side, and back down through the ladder 15º on the right side where you started. Pull the thread tight to join the 15ºs into a loop **(photo l)**.

12 Sew through the 15º, B, and 15º on the right side so the thread exits the 15º on the top right of the B. From right to left, sew through the crystal. Flip the work so the B is in the front and the thread exits the left side of crystal on the top. Stitch up through the 15º, B, and 15º on the left side, and then from the right to the left through the center 15º between the B and C **(photo m)**.

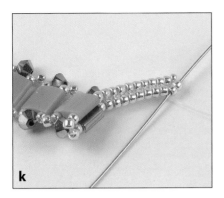

k

l

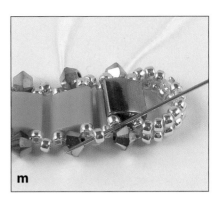

m

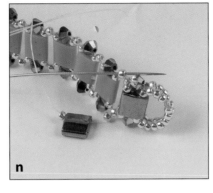

n

o

13 Pick up a 15º, a B, and a 15º, and sew from left to right through the top center 15º between the previous and new B **(photo n)**. This adds a new B and attaches it to the A.

14 Retrace the thread path through the previous 15º, B, and 15º **(photo o)**. Sew from right to left through the center 15º; up through the new 15º, B, and 15º; and from right to left through the top crystal.

15 Pick up a 15º, and sew down through the second hole of the new B. Pick up a 15º, and sew from left to right through the bottom crystal; up through the 15º, B, and 15º; from right to left through the top crystal; down through the 15º, B, and 15º; and from right to left through the bottom center 15º.

16 Repeat steps 13–15, adding Bs on top of all the As. End the final step with your thread exiting the bottom 15º of the B.

17 Turn the work so the As and Bs are side by side and the thread is exiting a 15º on the top left B. Work as in steps 9–13 to create the ladder-stitch loop. Sew through two or three 15ºs, and then reverse direction and sew through four 15ºs.

18 Tie a **half-hitch knot** (Technique Spotlight, p. 27), and sew through two more 15ºs. Tie another half-hitch knot, sew through a bead, and end the threads.

19 Slip a pearl enhancer clasp through one end ring.

TIP You can use a swivel lobster clasp instead of the pearl enhancer. Attach the clasp in step 10 after completing six ladder stitches by sewing through the lobster clasp swivel ring and then picking up two 15ºs and continuing in the ladder stitch pattern.

NECKLACE
Work the necklace exactly like the bracelet, except substitute 4mm crystals on the bottom edge to create a gentle curve. You will use about 62–70 Tilas on each side. The necklace should rest right on your collarbone.

71

Buttonhole
BRACELET AND PENDANT

CONVERT IT!

Place the focal clasp into the top buttonhole, wrap the bracelet around your wrist, and "button" through the bottom buttonhole—or switch the focals for a brand-new bracelet!

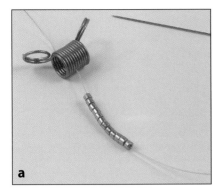

a

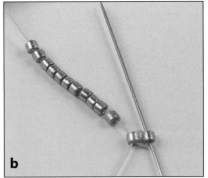

b

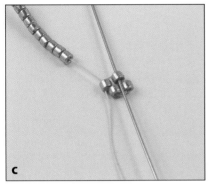

c

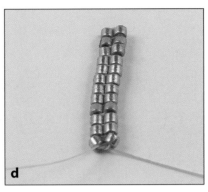

d

MATERIALS
- **Swarovski Elements**

  38mm crystal filigree
  (Article 62004)

  27mm crystal filigree
  (Article 62010)

  26mm crystal filigree
  (Article 62022)

  20mm vintage crystal button
  (Article 3818)

- 12 grams 11º cylinder seed beads

- beading thread (KO or One-G)

- ½-in. (1.3cm) flat shirt button

TOOLS
- size 11 or 12 beading needle

- sharp scissors or cutters

- beading mat

- bead stopper (optional)

Square stitch worked with cylinder beads makes a flexible wrist band. The buttonholes on each end allow you to swap out the filigree focal clasp. Try making a thinner version and wear the focals as pendants.

MAKE THE BRACELET

1 Thread a needle on a comfortable length of beading thread (about 1 yd./.9m). Add a **bead stopper** about 4 in. (10cm) from the end (Technique Spotlight, p. 19). Pick up 12 11º cylinder seed beads and slide them down to the bead stopper to begin working in **square stitch** (Technique Spotlight). This will be the foundation column. Hold the 11ºs in your non-dominant hand, with the bead stopper at the top **(photo a)**.

2 Pick up an 11º, and sew from the top down through the 12th 11º in the foundation column. This bead will align with the twelfth 11º as you pull the thread snug. Sew up through the new 11º **(photo b)**, and pull the thread snug.

3 Pick up an 11º, and sew from the top down through the next 11º in the foundation column (the eleventh bead). Pull the thread snug. The new 11º will align next to the foundation column and sit above the first 11º in the new column. Stitch up from the bottom of the new 11º **(photo c)**.

4 Repeat step 3 to complete the column. Turn the work over so the thread is now exiting the bottom of the work **(photo d)**.

5 Work as in steps 2 and 3 until you have a band long enough to fit around your wrist (or equals the exact wrist measurement), **ending** and **adding thread** as needed (Technique Spotlight, p. 37). My bracelet is 98 columns long.

TIP This bracelet is worked on the vertical side in columns of 12 beads.

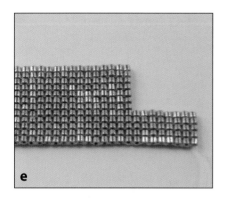

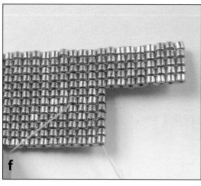

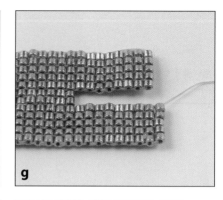

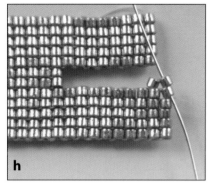

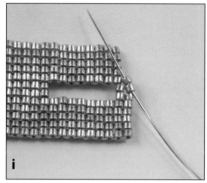

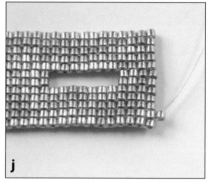

6 Work as in steps 2 and 3 eight more times, except only add five 11ºs to each new row **(photo e)**. Sew through a few rows of beads, and end the threads.

7 Thread a needle on a new length of thread (about 1 yd.), and sew through the two 11ºs in the center rows five columns back from the beginning of the buttonhole and then through the seven 11ºs. Turn the work, if necessary, so the thread is exiting the bottom of the row **(photo f)**.

8 Work as in steps 2 and 3 nine times, only adding five 11ºs to each new row, ending and adding thread as needed **(photo g)**.

9 Pick up two 11ºs, and sew down through the top 11º of the previous column and then up through the top 11º of the final column and the first new 11º **(photo h)**.

10 Pick up two 11ºs, sew down through the second new 11º added in the previous step, and sew up through the first new 11º added in this step.

11 Pick up an 11º, and sew down through the first 11º in the column above the buttonhole and the second 11º added in step 10. Then sew up through the first 11º added in step 10 and the 11º added in this step. This will begin to join the lower and upper sections of the buttonhole **(photo i)**.

12 Pick up an 11º, and sew down through the next 11º in the column and then up through the new 11º added in this step. Repeat, adding one 11º at a time, until you reach the top of the upper buttonhole section. Flip the work so the thread is exiting the 11º at the bottom.

13 Add two more columns of 11ºs. Flip the work so the thread is exiting the 11º at the bottom.

14 Sew up through two 11ºs to the left of the bottom 11º and then down through one 11º along the right edge. Pick up an 11º, and sew down through the next 11º in the previous column and up through the 11º added in this step **(photo j)**. This creates one decrease. Repeat, adding one 11º at a time, until you reach the next-to-last

11º on the column. This decreases one 11º on the top edge. Flip the work so the thread exits the 11º at the bottom.

15 Repeat step 14, except sew through three 11ºs to the left of the bottom 11º. This decreases two 11ºs along the bottom edge. Also decrease two 11ºs on the top edge. Sew through the beadwork and end the threads.

16 Remove the bead stopper, and add a new thread (about 1 yd.) to the beginning column of 11ºs where the first thread exits. Work as in steps 6–15 to make a corresponding buttonhole on this end of the bracelet. Tie the threads together, and sew through the beadwork to hide the knot. End the threads.

TIP When cutting thread close to the beadwork, lay your scissors or clippers flat against the work and pull the thread tight before cutting. The cut end will recede into the beadwork.

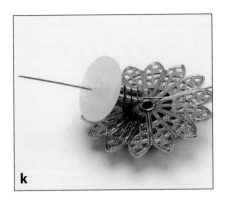

k

FILIGREE FOCAL BUTTON CLASPS

1 Make a square stitch rectangle five beads high and six columns across. Fold the piece at the three-bead column, and sew up through the first column of 11°s and back down the final column to join the sides.

2 Pick up the flat shirt button, and sew through one of the holes. If using a two-hole button, sew up through the second hole. If using a four-hole button, sew up through the opposite diagonal hole. Continue through one column of the square-stitch unit.

3 Sew up through a filigree space as close to the center as possible. Sew back down through the filigree, making sure the thread crosses one of the metal pieces and is underneath the raised crystal area **(photo k)**.

4 Sew down through the square-stitch unit and the button (in an unused hole if using a four-hole button or the first hole if using a two-hole button).

5 Sew up through the button, the square-stitch unit, and the filigree until all three pieces are secured together. Tie the thread off between the square-stitch unit and the button, and end the threads.

TIP Try using a vintage Swarovski button as a focal closure. If the button has a shank, you won't need to make the square-stitch unit; just stitch the two buttons loosely together. Assemble the bracelet just like the filigrees, with the crystal button on top of the band.

BUTTONHOLE PENDANT

Follow the steps for the Buttonhole Bracelet, except make the columns one bead high and 35 rows across. Don't decrease on the ends. Make the buttonhole sections the same size as for the bracelet. Wear the pendant by folding the pieces over your necklace and lining up the buttonholes. Attach the focal through both buttonholes to secure.

Square Stitch

1 String the required number of beads for the first row. Then pick up the first bead of the second row. Sew through the last bead of the first row and the first bead of the second row in the same direction as before. The new bead sits on top of the old bead, and the holes are parallel.

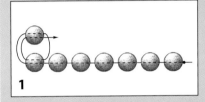

1

2 Pick up the second bead of row 2, and go through the next-to-last bead of row 1. Continue through the new bead in row 2. Repeat this step for the entire row.

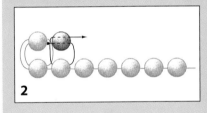

2

Peyote Pathway
BRACELET

CONVERT IT!

Choose crystals that match both solid-color sides, and flip the bracelet around completely to go from dark to light.

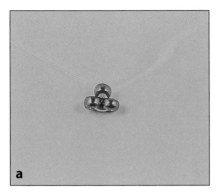

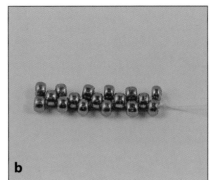

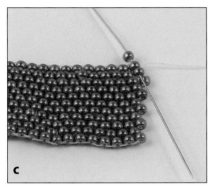

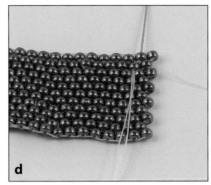

MATERIALS
- **Swarovski Elements**

    84 3mm Xilion (bicone) crystals (Article 5810)

- 10 grams $11^{\underline{o}}$ seed beads in each of **2** colors: A, B

- beading thread, 8 lb. test (Fireline)

- E hook style clasp

- nail polish (optional)

TOOLS
- **2** size 11 or 12 beading needles

- sharp scissors or cutters

- emery board (optionla)

- beading mat

TECHNIQUE SPOTLIGHT

Working in Odd-Count Peyote
To work all subsequent even-numbered rows, pick up one bead per stitch, exiting the end up-bead in the previous row **(a–b)**. To work all subsequent odd-numbered rows, pick up one bead per stitch, exiting the end up-bead in the previous row **(b–c)**. Pick up a bead, and sew under the thread bridge between the edge beads below **(c–d)**. Sew back through the last bead added to begin the next row **(d–e)**.

PREPARE THE CLASP
If you want the clasp to match the crystal color, try sanding it down with fine sandpaper (fingernail emery boards work well) and then painting it with nail polish. Paint a thin coat on one side, and when dry, flip over and paint a thin coat on the other side. Repeat for three coats total.

TWO-NEEDLE PEYOTE START
1 For **odd-count peyote** (Technique Spotlight), I like to start with a two-needle technique: Thread a needle on both ends of a comfortable length of thread. Pick up two color A $11^{\underline{o}}$ seed beads, and slide them to within 3–4 in. (7.6–10cm) of the second needle. Pick up an A with the second needle, and sew through the second A on the long end. Pull both threads tight to align with two beads on the bottom and one bead centered on top of the two **(photo a)**. This starts three rows.

2 Work as in step 1 for a total of 10 rows. Pick up an A on each needle, and tie the two threads together to make the 11th row **(photo b)**. Remove the needle from the short end.

STITCH IN ODD-COUNT PEYOTE
1 **Row 4:** Sew through one of the end As. Pick up an A, and sew through the next A in row 3. Continue the pattern of picking up an A and sewing through the next A four more times (this is a standard turn). Flip the work over so the thread exits a bottom A.

2 **Row 5:** Pick up an A, and sew through the next A from Row 4. Repeat four more times. Pick up an A, and sew down through the A on the top of the previous row and then through the A diagonally down and to the right **(photo c)**. Sew up through the A directly on the left and continue through the A on the diagonal right (stepped turn) **(photo d)**. Flip the work over so the thread is exiting the A at the bottom, and sew back up through the new A on the right.

3 Repeat steps 1 and 2, alternating between the standard and the stepped turns, until you have a band approximately ¾ in. (1.9cm) smaller than your wrist size, **ending** and **adding thread** as needed (Technique Spotlight, p. 37). Finish with a stepped turn. There should be "up" beads on both ends of the bracelet.

4 Pick up an A and sew through the next A four times, stopping short of the top edge. Pick up an A, and make a stepped turn in the next-to-last row **(photo e)**. This decreases one row. Turn the work over, pick up an A, and sew through the next A four times. Turn the work over, pick

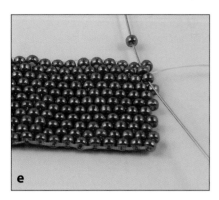

e

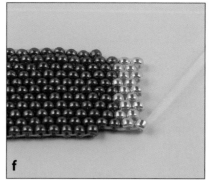

f

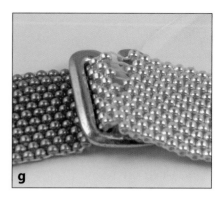

g

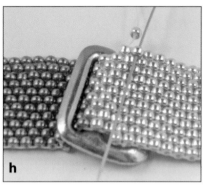

h

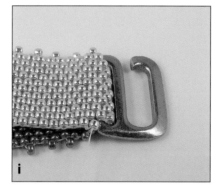

i

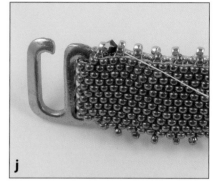

j

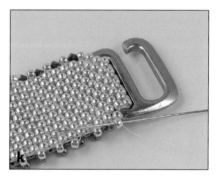

k

up an A, and sew through the next A four times. Pick up an A, and make a stepped turn.

5 Turn the work over and sew through the first A, work one row of peyote stitch using As, and work three more rows using color B 11º seed beads **(photo f)**. Add a new thread to the other side of the work, and repeat steps 4 and 5. End the threads and set the work aside.

6 With a new length of thread, work steps 1–5 using Bs until the bracelet is the same length as the A-color bracelet, minus the decreases. Do not cut the thread.

7 Pick up the A-color bracelet side, and slide the loop of the clasp over the decreased end. **Zip** (Techniques Spotlight, p. 55) the B end to the A end **(photo g)**. This will capture the clasp within the decreased edges. Sew through the edge bead of the first full-size B-color row.

8 Pick up a B, and sew through the next B on the edge of the bracelet **(photo h)**. Pull the thread snug so

the B lies perpendicular to the edge beads. Sew up through the next edge bead. Repeat this step to add Bs along one edge of the B-color side.

9 Zip the other decreased edge of the B-color band to the wide edge of the A-color band to create a loop for the hook of the clasp, and exit the edge bead of the first full-size row. Using As, repeat step 8 along the long edge of the A-color side. Finish with the thread exiting the bottom of the edge bead. Sew up through the first edge bead of the remaining B-color side **(photo i)**.

10 Repeat the edging technique in step 9, adding Bs to the B-color side. When you reach the end, sew up through the first edge bead of the remaining A-color band. Repeat the edging technique so you have A and B beads on all four edges. End by sewing up through the second edge bead, back through the first B on the edge, and then through an A on the edge.

11 Pick up a 3mm bicone crystal, and sew through the next A on the bracelet edge **(photo j)**. Repeat

for the remainder of the edge. End with the thread exiting the A on the edge. Sew through the B on the B side, and continue through the crystal and the next B. Repeat for the length of the bracelet.

12 Stitch through the band on the B side. Sew through the first edge bead on the B band and then through the B added in step 10 **(photo k)**. Pick up a crystal as in the previous step, and sew through the next B on the edge. Repeat all the way down the edge. Sew back through the A at the end, and then through the crystals and As all the way down the bracelet. End the threads.

Tila For Two x Two
BRACELET

CONVERT IT!

Flip this sturdy cuff inside out for another color option. Neutral beads complement striking shades.

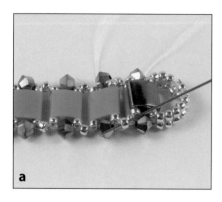

a

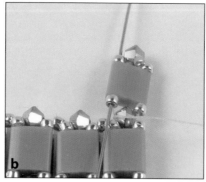

b

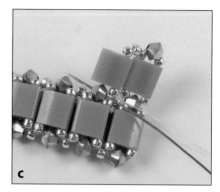

c

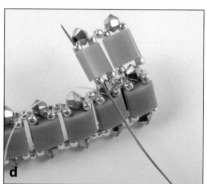

d

Refer to the "Tila for Two Bracelet and Necklace" to get started. This version is doubly beautiful!

BEGIN ROW 1

1 Work as in steps 1–8 of the "Tila For Two Bracelet," p. 68, using color A and B Tila beads, ending after adding the first B. **End** and **add thread** as needed (Technique Spotlight, p. 37).

2 Sew (from right to left) through the 3mm bicone crystal on the bottom of the B. Sew up through the 15º seed bead, B, and 15º on the left side, and then sew (from right to left) through the top center 15º between two color A Tila beads **(photo a)**.

3 Pick up a 15º, an B, and a 15º, and sew (from left to right) through the bottom center 15º between the previous and new B. This adds a new B and attaches it to the A.

4 Retrace the thread path through the previous 15º, B, and 15º, and sew (from right to left) through the center 15º, down through the new 15º, B, and 15º, and (from right to left) through the bottom crystal.

5 Pick up a 15º, and sew up through the new B. Pick up a 15º, and sew (from left to right) through the top crystal and down through the 15º, B, and 15º. Sew (from right to left) through the bottom crystal and back up through the 15º, B, and 15º. Then sew (from right to left) through the top center 15º.

6 Repeat steps 3–5, adding Bs on the top of all of the As. End the final step with the thread exiting the top 15º of the B.

ROW 2

TIP Using the smallest needle possible (size 12 or 13) will make it easier to pass through the 15ºs to stitch row 2.

1 Sew from left to right through the center crystal. Turn the work so the A is facing you, with the bracelet on the left side and the thread exiting the left side of the center crystal.

2 Pick up a 15º, an A, a 15º, a crystal, and a 15º. Sew down through the right hole of the A. Pick up a 15º, and sew (from right to left) through the crystal (which is now shared between the two rows of Tilas), and up through the 15º, A, and 15º added in this step **(photo b)**.

3 Pick up two 15ºs, an A, and a 15º. Sew (from left to right) through the center (shared) 15º in the first row, and sew up through the previous 15º, A, and 15º. Sew (from right to left) through the center (shared) 15º, and sew down through the 15º, A, and 15º added in this step. Sew (from right to left) through the shared crystal **(photo c)**.

4 Pick up a 15º, and sew through the left side of the A. Pick up a 15º and a crystal, and then sew down through the 15º, a A, and a 15º on the right side, and then sew (from right to left) through the shared crystal. Continue up through the left side 15º, A, and the first 15º added in this step **(photo d)**.

5 Repeat steps 3 and 4 across all the As in the first row. Finish with the thread exiting the top 15º on the left side. Flip the work so the Bs of the first row are in front and the thread is exiting the 15º above the rightmost A.

6 Pick up a 15º, a B, and a 15º. Sew up through the last 15º, A, and 15º, then down through the new 15º, B, and 15º added in this step. Sew (from right to left) through the shared crystal. Align the new B over the A **(photo e)**. Pick up a 15º, and sew up through the left side of the B. Pick up a 15º, and sew (from left to right) through the top crystal. To reposition the thread, sew through the 15º, B, and 15º on the right side, (from right to left) through the shared crystal, and up through the 15º, B, and 15º on the left side. Then sew (from right to left) through the middle

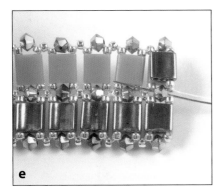

MATERIALS
- **Swarovski Elements**

  99 3mm Xilion bicone crystals (Article 5328) or round crystals (Article 5000)

- **66** Tila beads in each of **2** colors: A, B

- 6–7 grams 15º seed beads

- beading thread, 6 lb. test (Fireline)

TOOLS
- size 12 beading needle

- sharp scissors

- beading mat

15º on the top row between two As (shared top 15º).

7 Pick up a 15º, a B, and a 15º. Sew (from left to right) through the middle shared 15º, and back up through the previous 15º, B, and 15º. Sew (from right to left) through the top shared 15º, and continue through the new 15º, B, and 15º. Sew (from right to left) through the center row shared crystal.

8 Pick up a 15º, and sew up through the left side of the new B. Pick up a 15º, and sew (from left to right) through the top shared crystal. Sew down through the 15º, B, and 15º on the right side (from right to left) and through the shared crystal in the center row, and then sew up through the new 15º, B, and 15º. Position the thread by passing from right to left through the shared top 15º.

9 Repeat steps 7 and 8 to attach Bs to each A. Finish with the thread exiting the top-left 15º on the final B **(photo f)**.

CLASP LOOP

1 Turn the bracelet so the edges of the As and Bs are side by side and the thread is exiting the 15º on the right (on top of the B). Pick up two 15ºs, and sew down through the 15º, A, and 15º on the left. Align the two 15ºs so they rest on top of the first two 15ºs. Sew back up through the 15º, B, and 15º on the right side and through the first new 15º added in this step.

2 Make a ladder-stitch strip: Pick up two 15ºs, sew down through one 15º on the left side, and then sew back up through the 15º on the right and the first new 15º. Repeat this step 17 more times; the ladder will be 20 rows total, including the 15ºs directly above the two Tilas **(photo g)**.

3 Join the ladder-stitched 15ºs by sewing up through the 15º, B, and 15º on the opposite side, and then sewing down through the 15º, A, and 15º on the left side. Sew through the ladder-stitched 15º on the left side, and then sew back through the ladder-stitched 15º on the right side where you started. Pull the thread tight to join the 15ºs into a loop. Sew through

the 15º on the base of the B and then back down through the 15º on the base of the A. Continue through three or four 15ºs in the loop. Tie a half-hitch knot using just the threads between the beads, and sew through a few more 15ºs. End the threads.

MAKE THE TOGGLE

1 On a new length of thread (about 1 yd.), pick up a 15º, an A, a 15º, a crystal, and a 15º, leaving a 6-in. tail. Sew through the other side of the A, pick up a 15º and a crystal, and tie a square knot with the tail and working thread. Sew up through the 15º, A, and 15º.

2 Pick up a 15º, a B, and a 15º. Sew through the right-side 15º, A, and 15º, and then sew through the new 15º, B, and 15º **(photo h)**. Fold the B (from right to left) over the A, and sew (from right to left) through the bottom shared crystal. Pick up a 15º, and sew up through the left side of the B. Pick up a 15º, and sew (from left to right) through the top shared crystal.

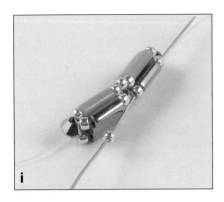

i

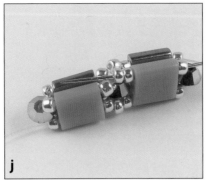

j

k

l

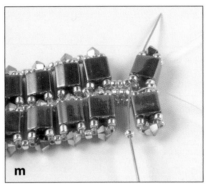

m

and sew through all of the 15ºs of one side of the ladder stitch added in this step.

9 Sew through the 15º, A, and 15º of the toggle, and then sew through the crystal and all the beads on the B side of the toggle, the crystal, and the 15º, B, and 15º **(photo l)**. Pick up a 15º, and sew through the next 15º, B, and 15º unit and through the shared crystal. Sew through all of the beads on the A side of the toggle, the shared crystal, and the 15º, A, and 15º. Pick up a 15º, and sew through the next 15º, B, and 15º unit **(photo m)**.

10 Retrace the thread path through the toggle beads once more (if possible) to stiffen the work. Tie a **half-hitch knot** (Technique Spotlight, p. 27) between two beads, and end the threads.

3 Pick up a 15º, a B, a 15º, a crystal, and a 15º. Sew down though the left side of the B, pick up a 15º, and sew (from left to right) through the shared crystal. Continue up through the 15º, B, and 15º on the right. Sew (from right to left) through the top shared crystal, and flip the work over so that the bottom A is in the front and the thread exits the crystal on the right side.

4 Pick up a 15º, an A, and a 15º, and sew (from right to left) through the shared crystal (which now makes it the center shared crystal). Pick up a 15º, and sew up though the left side of the A. Pick up a 15º, and sew from left to right through the top shared crystal and down through the 15º, A, and 15º.

5 Pick up a 15º, and sew through the 15º, A, and 15º on the bottom and then up through the bottom 15º, B, and 15º on the other side. Pick up a 15º, and sew through the top 15º, B, and 15º **(photo i)**.

6 Pick up two 15ºs, and sew through the 15º, A, and 15º on the top. Then sew back down through the 15º, B, and 15º on the top and through the first 15º added in this step **(photo j)**.

7 Begin to create a strip of ladder stitch that is two beads wide and four rows long **(photo k)**. Once you have finished the ladder, keeping the B sides of both the toggle and the bracelet facing up, sew through the 15º, B, and 15º unit on the bracelet. Sew back through the 15º, A, and 15º unit on the other side. Sew through all of the 15ºs in the ladder stitch on the same side, and then sew through the 15º, A, and 15º, the crystal, all of the beads on the A side, the crystal, and the 15º, B, and 15º.

8 Add matching rows of ladder stitch on the other side, and sew up through the 15º, B, and 15º in the bracelet end. Sew back down through the 15º, A, and 15º in the bracelet end,

Double Lattice
BRACELET

CONVERT IT!

Wear this reversible bracelet to set off two different outfits. A large crystal pearl clasp closes seamlessly with either color.

a

b

c

d

e

f

This double-sided bracelet starts with a pearl base and is embellished with two different netting patterns and seed bead colors.

MAKE THE BRACELET

1 Thread the beading elastic onto the twisted wire needle. Pick up 10 3mm pearls, and sew through all the 3mms to make a ring, leaving a 6-in. (15cm) tail. Pull snug **(photo a)**. Tie a **surgeon's knot** (Technique Spotlight, p. 19), and pull tight. Sew through an adjacent 3mm, and pull the knot into it. Trim both ends of the elastic close to the 3mm.

2 Thread a beading needle with a comfortable length of Fireline (about 1 yd./.9m), and using a simple **overhand knot** (Technique Spotlight, p. 13), tie the tail end onto the circle of 3mms you made in step 1, so it lays between two 3mms **(photo b)**.

3 Pick up three 3mms, loop the thread between the next two 3mms in the elastic ring, and then sew back through the last 3mm added in this

step **(photo c)**. Pick up two 3mms, loop the thread between the next two 3mms in the elastic ring, and then sew back through the last 3mm added in this step **(photo d)**. This builds the foundation row for the right-angle weave stitches to follow.

4 Sew through the first 3mm in the two-3mm foundation row, and then work **right-angle weave** (Technique Spotlight, p. 49) until you have completed at least 38 rows, **ending** and **adding thread** as needed (Technique Spotlight, p. 37). Count the 3mms on one long side of the bracelet to determine the number of rows you have worked. The bracelet should be about ¼ in. (6mm) longer than your usual bracelet length.

TIP In the foundation rows, notice that one row has three 3mms across and the other row has two 3mms across. To make a longer bracelet, add rows in groups of four (two rows of two 3mms each, two rows of three 3mms each) so the larger diamond pattern is even.

5 With the thread exiting between the final two 3mms of the last row, bring the loose thread end down past the 3mm where the thread is exiting, and reposition the needle. This doubles the thread for the next few steps.

6 Pick up the 10mm crystal pearl and a 3mm. Sew back down through the 10mm in the band **(photo e)**, and then through the top 3mm on the right side of the two-3mm row. Sew around through each of the 3mms in the right-angle weave unit and up through the center 3mm of the three-3mm row **(photo f)**.

MATERIALS

- **Swarovski Elements**

  crystal pearls (Article 5810)

  10mm

  210 3mm

- **40–50** 11º seed beads, color B

- 15º seed beads

  3 grams color A

  1 gram color B

- beading thread, 8 lb. test (Fireline)

- 6 in. Stretch Magic beading elastic, 0.5mm

TOOLS

- twisted wire beading needle

- size 11 or 12 beading needle

- sharp scissors or cutters

- beading mat

7 Sew through the 10mm, the 3mm, and down through the 10mm, then through the top 3mm on the left side of the two-3mm row. Sew around through the right angle-weave unit, and up through the center 3mm of the three-3mm row.

8 Repeat, sewing up through the 10mm and 3mms and back down through the 10mm one more time. Wrap the thread around the base threads of the 10mm-3mm, and tie two **half-hitch knots** (Technique Spotlight, p. 27). Cut ONE thread with sharp scissors, and reposition the needle so you are now working with a single thread **(photo g)**.

9 Pick up a color A 15º seed bead, and sew through the center 3mm in the first three-3mm row. Pick up an A and sew through the 3mm in the next three-3mm row. Keeping a smooth tension, repeat through the length of the bracelet, exiting the final 3mm in a three-3mm row.

10 Pick up an A, loop the thread around the elastic between the center two 3mms in the clasp, and then sew from right to left through the 3mm on the left **(photo h)**. Keeping a smooth tension, add an A between each of the 3mms on the outside row.

11 After adding the final A, smooth the bracelet to make sure the threads aren't pulled too tight. Check for fit, and loosen or tighten the side beads if needed. Sew through the top 3mm in the two-3mm row, wrap the thread around the base of the 10mm-3mm, and sew through the next 3mm in the two-3mm row. Work as in step 10, adding As between the 3mms on the remaining side.

12 Smooth the tension as in step 11. Attach the final A by looping the thread around the elastic (between two 3mms), and then sew through the top 3mm so the thread exits above the center 3mm and A. Sew through the first A in the center row.

13 Pick up five As, and sew through the next A in the center row. Repeat this step for the length of the bracelet **(photo i)**. After sewing through the final A, wrap the thread around the stem of the 10mm, and sew back through the same A. Turn the work around, pick up five As, and sew through the A in the center row. Continue adding five As down the center of the bracelet **(photo j)**. After adding the final five As, sew through the 3mm on the elastic ring and through the first A on the edge.

19 Pick up a B, and sew through the 3mm on the outside edge as in step 17. Repeat this step until you have added a B between each 3mm on the outside edge. After sewing through the final 3mm, pick up a B and sew through the 3mm in the end two-3mm row. Wrap the thread around the base of the 10mm, and sew down through the first B in the middle row.

20 Pick up five Bs, and sew through the second B on one of the long edges. Pick up five Bs, and sew through the next B (skipping the 11º) in the middle row **(photo m)**. Repeat, picking up five Bs and sewing through the edge Bs (skipping one edge B) and then picking up five Bs and sewing through the next center B (skipping the 11º) for the length of the bracelet. Sew through the center B in the clasp end, and turn the work.

21 Repeat step 20 along the remaining outside edge, and using the same middle row bead used for the first edge. You will create a large diamond shape with the 11º in the center.

22 Finish by sewing through the middle B, and then wrap the thread around the 10mm post and through the first three segments of the diamond shape. Tie two half-hitch knots, sew through a few more Bs, tie another knot, sew through a few more Bs, and end the threads. Weave any tail ends into the adjacent beads, and trim the threads close.

14 Pick up two As, and sew through the middle A of the five-bead unit added in step 13 **(photo k)**. Pick up two As, and sew through the next A that lies between two 3mms on the edge of the bracelet **(photo l)**. This will make a diamond shape.

15 Repeat step 14 for the length of the bracelet. After adding the final two As, sew through the end 3mm, wrap the thread around the base of the 10mm-3mm as before, and then sew through the next end 3mm and the first A. Work as in step 14 along the remaining edge of the bracelet.

16 Attach the final two As by sewing through the last A on the bracelet edge, and then sewing through the center of the elastic clasp to the opposite side.

17 Pick up a color B 15º seed bead, and sew through the 3mm on an outside edge. Repeat for the length of the bracelet. At the end of the row, pick up a B and sew through the 3mm on the two-3mm row, wrap thread around the base of the 10mm, pick up a B, and sew through the center 3mm in the three-3mm row.

18 Pick up an 11º seed bead, and sew through the next 3mm in the middle row. Continue for the length of the bracelet, alternately adding a B and an 11º. At the end of the row, pick up a B, and sew through the 3mm in the elastic ring toward the outer edge that hasn't been embellished.

CONVERT IT!

Flip this reversible bracelet for a completely different colorway. One side even has a bit of extra embellishment.

Back-to-Back
FLATBACKS
BRACELET

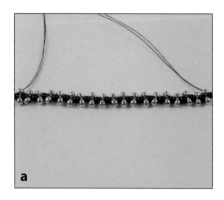

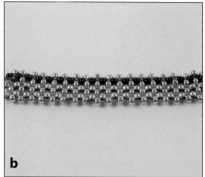

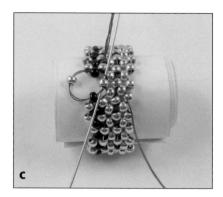

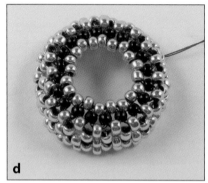

Right-angle weave units are beaded using flatback crystals and seed beads. The toggle closure is created in the same way, and the units are all then connected. An optional version uses tiny 2mm round Swarovski beads in place of some of the seed beads for even more sparkle and opulence!

MAKE THE FLATBACK MEDALLIONS

Each back-to-back medallion unit is woven individually and then connected together. Prepare the flatbacks by using ¼-in. (6mm) sections of double-sided tape or a bit of jewelry glue to join one color A and one color B flatback together.

1 Thread a needle on a comfortable length of beading thread (about 1 yd./.9m), and pick up a color A 11º seed bead, a color B 11º seed bead, an A 11º, and a B 11º. Form the 11ºs into a circle, and tie a knot, leaving a 2–3-in. (5–7.6cm) tail. Keeping the knot and tail on the left side, sew through the first B 11º, the A 11º, and the second B 11º. Work a row of **right-angle weave** (Technique Spotlight, p. 49) that has 19 A 11ºs across the top and bottom rows and 20 B 11ºs across the center. Sew through the next A 11º **(photo a)**.

2 Using only A 11ºs, work two more rows of right-angle weave **(photo b)**. Sew through the next A 11º on the short edge. Join the short sides together: Pick up an A 11º, sew through the corresponding edge on the other end, pick up an A 11º, and sew through the A 11º your thread exited at the start of this step. Continue through the first A 11º added in this step and the next edge A 11º in the previous row. Pick up an A 11º, and sew through the corresponding A 11º on the first edge. Continue through the next three A 11ºs in this right-angle

weave unit, and then sew through the edge B 11º in the first row. Pick up an A 11º, and sew through the edge B 11º on the other edge, Pick up an A 11º, and retrace the thread path through the B 11º , A 11º, B 11º, and A 11º in this stitch. This will create a right-angle weave tube **(photo c)**.

3 Sew through all of the A 11ºs along the edge of the tube, and pull snug so that the 11ºs lie close to each other and form a smooth circle. Retrace the thread path several times to secure **(photo d)**.

4 In a zigzag fashion (so that you don't cross through any of the right-angle weave intersections), sew through the beadwork to the second long side of the tube. Sew through all of the A 11ºs on this edge of the tube as in step 4, but do not pull snug yet.

5 Position a back-to-back flatback in the tube, with the color B side facing against the B 11ºs. Tighten the thread as you did in step 5, and retrace the thread path to secure **(photo e)**. Stitch through the beads in a zigzag

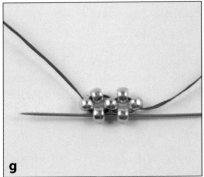

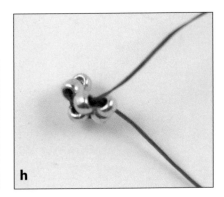

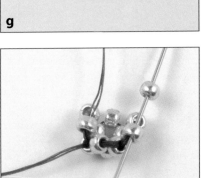

fashion to secure the thread. **End the threads** (Technique Spotlight, p. 37).

6 Repeat steps 1–5 to make a total of eight flatback medallions.

MAKE THE TOGGLE CLASP

1 To make the round portion of the toggle clasp, work as in step 1, but make the piece with 22 horizontal A 11°s and 23 vertical B 11°s. Work as in steps 2 and 3 to add two more rows of right-angle weave using A 11°s, and join to form a tube.

2 Work as in steps 4–6, but don't place a back-to-back medallion in the tube **(photo f)**.

3 Stitch in and out between the two tightened edges (which are now the inner circles) to secure the beads together. Stitch through the beads in a zigzag fashion to secure the thread and meet the tail. Tie the two ends together, secure through a few beads, and end the threads.

4 To make the cubic right-angle weave toggle portion of the clasp, begin by making two regular right-angle weave units with A 11°s. Sew through both bottom A 11°s **(photo g)**. Tip the unit on the right side up so it sits at a 90-degree angle to the left-side unit. Two of the A 11°s in this unit will be vertical and the top A 11° of the unit will be horizontal. Position the work so the needle and thread are on the right side and the tipped-up unit is on the left **(photo h)**.

5 Pick up two A 11°s, and sew from top to bottom through the vertical A 11° in the second unit, sew through the horizontal A 11°s (from left to right), and then sew through the next horizontal A 11°. Repeat this step once more.

6 Sew upward through the vertical A 11° on the right side. Pick up an A 11°, and sew downward through the vertical A 11° on the left side **(photo i)**. Pull the threads tight. You have created a right-angle weave cube.

7 Sew through the horizontal A 11° on the right, the vertical A 11° to the right of that, and the horizontal A 11° on the top of the cube.

MATERIALS
- **Swarovski Elements**

  8 14mm chessboard circle flatback crystals (Article 2035) in each of **2** colors: A, B

- 11° seed beads, 46 grams in color A and 2 grams in color B

- beading thread, 6 lb. test (Fireline)

- strong double-sided tape (optional) or beading glue

TOOLS
- size 11 or 12 beading needle

- sharp scissors or cutters

- beading mat

j

k

l

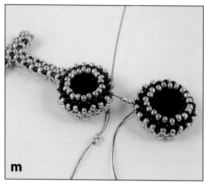

m

8 Work all subsequent rows by picking up three new A 11ºs and sewing from left to right through the same A 11º that the thread exits. Sew (from left to right) through the next A 11º on the top of the previous cube **(photo j)**. Pick up two new A 11ºs, and sew down through the vertical A 11º to the left, and sew (from left to right) through the horizontal A 11º where the thread exited. Sew from left to right through the next A 11º on the top of the previous cube. Pick up two A 11ºs, sew down through the vertical A 11º to the left, and sew (from left to right) through the horizontal A 11º where the thread exited. Sew (from left to right) through the next A 11º on the top of the previous cube, and sew up through the horizontal A 11º on the right. Pick up a new A 11º, and sew down through the vertical A 11º on the left, the horizontal A 11º in the base, the horizontal A 11º on the right, and (from left to right) through the horizontal A 11º on the top.

9 Complete five cubic right-angle weave rows for the cross section of the toggle. Reposition the thread to exit a horizontal A 11º three rows from one edge. Your thread should exit the right side of the bead. Pick up three A 11ºs, and work a cubic right-angle weave unit using the toggle cross section as the base for the cubic right-angle weave.

10 Work four or five more cubic right-angle weave units for the toggle stem **(photo k)**.

CONNECT THE MEDALLIONS AND CLASP

1 Connect the toggle to the edge of a medallion by continuing the cubic right-angle weave pattern, except only pick up one new A 11º and sew through one A 11º in the center row of the medallion **(photo l)**. Pick up one new A 11º and sew through the original bead on the toggle edge, and then sew through the next A 11º on the toggle edge. Connect all four sides of the toggle stem, and then sew in a zigzag manner halfway around the medallion. Position the thread to exit a horizontal A 11º in the center row of the right-angle weave.

2 Connect the next medallion by picking up two A 11ºs and sewing through the corresponding A 11º in a new medallion. Pick up two A 11ºs, and sew through the first A 11º on the first medallion **(photo m)**. Retrace the thread path once or twice through all the beads to secure. If enough thread remains on your needle, sew through the side of the medallion in a zigzag manner as before to add a new medallion. Otherwise, end the thread and begin a new thread at the opposite side of the medallion.

3 Connect all the medallions in the same manner. Finish by connecting the toggle ring the same way you connected the medallions together: Pick up a new A 11º, sew through a center A 11º in the toggle ring, and then pick up a new A 11º and sew through the original A 11º on the medallion. Reinforce the beads: Retrace the thread path through all of the beads, and then sew through a few beads in a zigzag manner. End the threads.

TIP To add length without adding a medallion, pick up three or four beads in step 2 to connect the medallions.

The Ultimate
LARIAT-AND-BRACELET

CONVERT IT!

To wear the shorter, simple necklace, connect the two bead-cap ends. Add the bracelet and the necklace together to make a longer necklace. Add tassel ends for the most luxurious look.

a

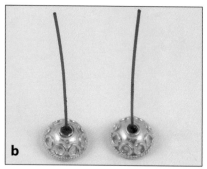

b

c

d

e

f

The ultimate in crystal abundance, this project uses more than one thousand crystal beads to make a necklace and bracelet that can be mixed and matched in multiple ways.

MAKE THE CLASPS

1 Divide the magnets into four pairs. Mark the outside of each pair with a permanent marker or a bit of nail polish for reference.

2 Mix the two-part epoxy clay according to the manufacturer's instructions, and roll a very small ball (a little smaller than pea-size). Place a ball in a bead cap, and press to fill the space. Place the marked side of the magnet onto the clay, and push a headpin through the magnet, the clay, and then the bead cap hole (**photo a**).

3 Smooth the epoxy clay around the bead cap and clean off any clay that oozes out or covers the magnet. Place the bead cap on the non-adhesive side of a piece of tape on a hard surface, and slide it around a bit to make sure the clay surface is smooth (**photo b**). If necessary, clean up any exposed clay. Make a total of six bead caps.

4 When the clay has cured for a few hours, remove it from the tape and clean off any excess clay. When fully cured, make a **wrapped loop** (Technique Spotlight, p. 40) with the headpin (**photo c**).

Change It Up!

Attach the tassel ends to another set of bead cap clasps, and hang on a pair of earring wires for fun and flirty earrings.

MAKE THE NECKLACE AND BRACELET

1 Thread a needle on a comfortable length of beading thread (about 1 yd./.9m), and make a two-unit strip of **right-angle weave** (Technique Spotlight, p. 49), using four 4mm bicone crystals for the first unit and three 4mm bicones for the second unit. Sew through all three new crystals in the second unit, and then sew through the top crystal of the first unit.

2 Tip the second unit up so it sits at a 90-degree angle to the first unit. Two of the beads in this second unit will be vertical, and the top bead will be horizontal. Position the work so the needle and thread are on the right side and the tipped-up unit is on the left (**photo d**).

3 Pick up two 4mm bicone crystals, and sew (from top to bottom) through the vertical bead in the second unit. Continue through the horizontal bead (from left to right), and then sew through the next horizontal bead. Repeat this step once.

4 Sew through the vertical crystal on the right side. Pick up a crystal, sew downward through the vertical crystal

on the left side **(photo e)**, and pull the threads tight. You have created a right-angle weave cube.

5 Position the thread for the next row: Sew through the next horizontal crystal to the right and the next vertical crystal to the right, and then sew through the next horizontal crystal on the top of the cube.

6 Repeat steps 1–4 until your cubic right-angle weave rope measures 25 in. (64cm), **adding** and **ending thread** as needed (Technique Spotlight, p. 37). End with the thread exiting a horizontal crystal on the top.

7 Pick up the wrapped loop on one of the bead caps, and sew through the horizontal crystal opposite the crystal the thread is exiting. Sew back through the wrapped loop and the first crystal, making an "X" with the threads passing through the clasp loop **(photo f)**. Sew through the clasp loop, the crystal on the right side of the clasp, the clasp loop, and then the crystal on the left side of the clasp. Repeat this step one more time to make sure the clasp is secure.

8 Make one more round of cubic right-angle weave around the wrapped stem of the clasp. End with the thread exiting a horizontal crystal on the top **(photo g)**. Sew through the four crystals on the top two or three times to tighten them around the clasp. Sew down through one of the vertical crystals.

9 Working down the rope, pick up an 11º cylinder seed bead, and sew through the next vertical crystal **(photo h)**. Repeat for the length of the rope.

10 Work as in steps 7 and 8 to attach the other half of the clasp, then work as in step 9 to add 11ºs to the remaining sides of the rope.

11 Tie a **half-hitch knot** (Technique Spotlight, p. 27) between the right-angle weave units. Sew through a few crystals, tie another half-hitch knot, and end the thread.

12 Repeat steps 1–11 to make another 8–9 in. (20–23cm) rope for the bracelet. (Add at least 1 in./2.5cm to your regular wrist length for this measurement for ease.)

MATERIALS
- **Swarovski Elements**

  1100 4mm bicone crystals (Article 5328)
- 2 grams 11º cylinder seed beads
- **6** 14mm bead caps
- **8** ¼x⅛ in. disk-style magnets with ¹⁄₁₆-in. holes
- **24** 2-in. (5cm) headpins
- 3 in. (7.6cm) 22-gauge craft wire
- 6 in. (15cm) tape
- beading thread, 8 lb. test (Fireline)
- 2-part epoxy clay

TOOLS
- size 10, 11, or 12 beading needle
- roundnose pliers
- chainnose pliers
- wire cutters
- permanent marker or nail polish

MAKE THE TASSELS

1 String a crystal on each remaining headpin, and make a **wrapped loop** (Technique Spotlight, p. 40). Make a total of 16 crystal dangles.

2 String 96 crystals onto the roll of 22-gauge wire.

3 Wrap the wire end around your roundnose pliers to make a simple loop. Position the crystal close to the loop, and bend the wire 90 degrees. Make another loop with your round-nose pliers at this bend, and trim the wire close to the crystal. Repeat this step to make a total of 96 loop units.

4 **Open a loop unit** (Technique Spotlight, p. 15) and connect it to a crystal dangle loop. Close the loop. Connect five more simple loop units in a row, and connect the last loop to the wrapped loop of one clasp end. Repeat to make eight tassel ends on each side of a bead-cap clasp.

Acknowledgments

So very many people have helped me through this book-writing process, but none so much as the Kalmbach team: Thank you Erica Swanson, Lisa Schroeder, Bill Zuback, Dianne Wheeler, and Jami Rinehart.

Thank you, thank you, thank you!

The Create Your Style team at Swarovski; you changed my life and I will be eternally grateful.

Thank you Nicole Harper and Kim Paquette.

Thank you Linda and Tim Hartung at Alacarte Claps and Wire Lace for your generosity and encouragement.

Brenda Schweder…because you told me I could do it!

And to my Sparkle Sisters and a Mister….thank you all for your friendship, support, giggles, and sparkles.

About the Author

Diane Whiting is an award-winning designer who creates and teaches innovative jewelry and accessories featuring SWAROVSKI ELEMENTS. Her woven crystal purses have won numerous awards, including first place in the CREATE YOUR STYLE Design Contest 2006 Amateur Category.

In 2009, Diane was named one of the original CREATE YOUR STYLE with SWAROVSKI ELEMENTS Ambassadors. Her work has been published in *Bead&Button* magazine as well as many other major magazines.

Diane delights in teaching multiple techniques to both new and experienced bead enthusiasts and teaches at many notable bead shows, bead societies and bead stores around the country.

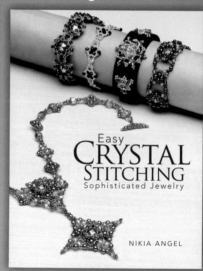
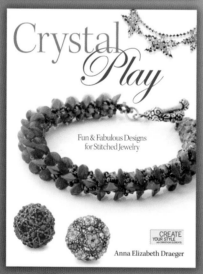
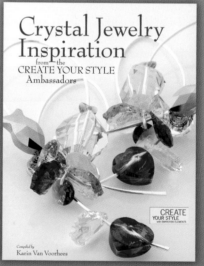